Cyber Security

Cyber Security

Edward Amoroso

SILICON PRESS
Summit, NJ 07901
www.silicon-press.com

Silicon Press, Summit, NJ 07901, USA
ISBN 0-929306-38-4
First Edition
Printing 9 8 7 6 5 4 3 2 1   Year 09 08 07 06

Library of Congress Cataloging-in-Publication Data

Amoroso, Edward G.
  Cyber security / Edward Amoroso.
    p. cm.
  Includes index.
  ISBN 0-929306-38-4 (alk. paper)
  1. Information warfare--United States. 2. Computer networks--Security measures--United States. 3. Cyberspace--Security measures. 4. Cyberterrorism--United States--Prevention. 5. Civil defense--United States. I. Title.

U163.A525 2007
363.325--dc22   2006005166

Contents

Preface

T HE BOOK YOU HAVE IN YOUR HANDS began its life seven years ago as a thick technical volume with an imposing title: *Protecting Critical Infrastructure from Cyber Attack*. As in my previous books, it contained obscure references, detailed technical charts, complex network diagrams, and sketched algorithms. The basic message in the book seemed fine, but I wasn't happy with the complicated treatment. I'd have been lucky if fifty people had bothered to read it, so I scrapped the entire thing.

Soon after, on the advice and urging of my wife, I took a deep breath and tried to rewrite the book for a more general, non-technical audience. The result was a bumpy second manuscript, entitled *Blindsided*. It was written in the years after the World Trade Center and Pentagon attacks. When I thumb through that manuscript now, I am taken by how seriously the 9/11 event affected my thinking.

The book was a bitter call to arms for the American government to wake up to the dangers of cyber terrorism. Every sentence sounded like I was shouting at someone. ("The global community *needs* to take *immediate* and *aggressive* action or the critical infrastructure will *collapse* in a tangle of cyber *rubble!*") I put this aside and decided to take some time to smell the roses.

More recently, in my work at AT&T, I found myself regularly trying to explain the intricacies of cyber security to our massive customer base. During a typical week in the past couple of years, I might find myself speaking with well over a dozen major customers about cyber security. And their interests were intensely practical.

They wanted to understand what sort of cyber security problems they should be considering. They wanted to know how hackers break into networks. They wanted to know what security methods would prove useful and cost-effective. And more than anything else, they wanted to know what to tell their senior leadership about a global cyber security problem that appeared to be growing with no bounds.

Thankfully, these customers included, and continue to include, both technical and non-technical people, spanning just about every country, culture, industry, and government sector one could possibly imagine. Thus, I was forced to think through my approach *very carefully*. And through endless hours lecturing and listening to these fine individuals, images of how to properly explain cyber security concepts began to sharpen in my mind. Occasionally, an analogy would bring an expression of understanding to someone's face – and I would take note of this, and reuse the analogy later.

Finally, when I sat down to put these ideas, analogies, and concepts to paper, I was surprised as they flowed from my fingers more easily than anything I'd ever written before. The result is this book. It is intended to be of use to you in your personal and professional life by making you more aware of an issue that far too few people understand or even recognize. It is written to change the way you think about software, computers, networks, and infrastructure. I hope it accomplishes that goal.

References and Bibliography

Throughout this book, references are made to situations, claims, and reports made over the years related to cyber security. Since this is not intended as a scholarly work, but rather as a mainstream introduction to help people understand cyber security, I've decided to leave the long list of references out.

If you are using this book as the basis for research, I'd first recommend otherwise; but if you are nonetheless determined to check on some claim made here, then please drop me a note at eamoroso@att.com and I will do my best to accommodate your research needs. I might add that with the accuracy and scope of most search engines, especially Google, listing printed references in a mainstream work seems unnecessary.

My decision to omit a bibliography stems more from the fact that virtually no books exist today that do an acceptable job of treating cyber security for non-technical readers. This lies in stark contrast to the sheer *number* of books that purport to explain cyber security to the masses. On my last visit to the local bookstore, I counted no less than four entire *shelves* of recently published books on various topics related to cyber security. When my first book on security came out in 1994 (*Fundamentals of Computer Security Technology*, Prentice Hall), there were only two other books on the topic that had been written – ever.

Nevertheless, if this book interests you, and you want more, then I suggest you consider any of Bruce Schneier's books. Marcus Ranum is another writer and expert worth looking up, as is Dorothy Denning. And in a pinch, you can always look up my own previous writings.

Acknowledgements

Over the past twenty-one years, my involvement with the cyber security community of AT&T, and now SBC, has provided a vantage point like no other in the world.

This fine group of individuals serves to protect the networks and infrastructure of one of the largest carriers in the world. Whether doing research, development, or staying up all night trying to diagnose a hacking problem, my involvement with this group is the reason I can fill up an entire book with ideas. The several hundreds of names of people associated with this center are far too numerous to mention, and I wouldn't dare mention one without the other. Thanks to you all.

My wife Lee offered support and guidance throughout this project, the fourth book she has had to endure. But unlike previous books, this one has her fingerprints all over it, and for this I offer my sincere gratitude. In these past eight years since my last book, in addition to Stephanie (now 13) and Matt (now 11), we've added our third child, Alicia (now 6). All three kids have been wonderful and respectful in giving Dad time between their school, sports, and dance activities to sit down to write.

I'd also like to express my gratitude to Narain Gehani for helping this project along. Not only is he a skilled editor, but he is also a world-class computer scientist. His experiences at Bell Labs, and his years of experience in computing contributed immeasurably to the successful completion of this book.

Finally, my colleagues and students at the Stevens Institute of Technology in Hoboken, New Jersey deserve mention. My involvement at the university teaching cyber security to undergraduates and graduates for nearly seventeen years has been an invaluable element in my own learning. Stevens is clearly a school on a dramatic rise in the global spotlight, especially as it expands its pure and applied research base. I'm as proud to be part of the Stevens Institute community as anything in my professional career.

E.A.
Andover, NJ

1 An Introduction To Cyber Security

E VERYONE SEEMS TO BE TALKING about cyber security these days. Unfortunately, most of this talk involves people complaining endlessly about some nagging or infuriating problem with a computer system. See if any of the following situations are familiar to you:

- Your home computer is so filled with viruses that you barely know what it will do next (other than crash). You rectify the situation by buying a new computer.

- You gasp as some expert reports that his Internet connection is attacked ten million times a day – and someone seated next to you shrugs, saying that this number sounds too low.

- All day at work, you're forced to fumble around with tokens, passwords, PINs, firewalls, and anti-virus software, but visitors can just snap their laptops directly into the company network.

- An article in the company newsletter reports that the security team invested huge money in an anti-Spam system, but you still get dozens of email invitations to improve your mortgage rate and meet girls.

- You try to find a decent book that will help you understand cyber security, but you can't find anything that weighs less than a bowling ball.

The purpose of this book is to provide a gentle, non-technical introduction to the complex topic of cyber security. It includes no diagrams, no equations, and no math. It is intended to make you a more informed citizen, a better businessperson, and perhaps an improved legislator – at least on matters related to cyber security.

The book is written for the bank manager in Chicago who asked me whether she should be encrypting her customer data (my answer was maybe). It is written for the non-technical civilian agency employee who asked during a recent security symposium how hackers really get into Web sites (my answer was easily). It is written for the retail store manager from the UK who pulled me aside to complain about his intrusion detection systems. ("They don't seem to be detecting any intrusions," he reported.)

It is also written for the innocent, but misinformed citizens around the world who have no idea how vulnerable we all are to cyber attack. These citizens need to understand that immediate action is required by business and government leaders to secure our global infrastructure. Citizens also need to recognize that the next generation – our children – will become more vulnerable to this cyber security threat if we do not take forceful action now.

What is Cyber Security?

Here's a working definition: Cyber Security involves reducing the risk of malicious attack to software, computers, and networks. This includes the tools used to detect break-ins, stop viruses, block malicious access, enforce authentication, enable encrypted communications, and on and on.

Cyber security has become such a huge issue recently, because the risk associated with most cyber attacks is simply too high. This high risk stems primarily – in the opinion of this author – from a lack of proper engineering focus in the design, development, and operation of the cyber systems we all use. Stated more bluntly: Our software, computers, and networks have been built so poorly, that cracking them is a big yawn.

Consider, by way of contrast, the intense engineering focus used to construct transportation bridges. Engineers know that the first step in building a bridge involves the development of a complex mathematical model. The size and shape of the bridge, together with estimates of material strengths, are all worked into the model to ensure proper functioning under every possible condition.

Next, the physical building blocks and materials for the bridge are selected. All steel and cables must be confirmed to have certain properties, so that when the bridge is constructed, it meets its specifications correctly. Finally, the actual construction has to be supervised by professional engineers, because shoddy workmanship can result in deaths.

The result of this engineering focus is that bridges are generally built pretty well, and it is rare that one buckles. Sure, a terrorist can explode a bomb on a bridge, but this is an inherent risk in any structure. What terrorists cannot do is exploit some flaw, bug, or vulnerability to intentionally topple a bridge. For example, you can't just yank on some flawed cable to make a bridge fall down – even in New York (sorry, I couldn't resist).

Furthermore, there are no remote attacks that can be attempted against a given bridge. For example, an evil hacker in Paris can't just push some button to take out the George Washington Bridge. The only real attacks that can be directed at a bridge are ones that are physical in nature – like a bomb or a missile – or ones that require the presence of the attacker near the bridge.

Unfortunately, none of these engineering considerations are true for the software, computers, and networks that exist across the globe. You might be surprised to know that software is rarely designed using mathematical models, or for that matter, much engineering thinking at all. We see the effects of this regularly, as the software and computer systems we use every day, fail miserably before our very eyes. When this happens to your computer, you say that it has crashed.[1] Computer software, in particular, is not developed to formal specifications, and as a result, it often requires persistent patching just to remain operational.

Worst of all, unlike bridges, cyber components can be intentionally attacked from remote locations. That is, a malicious person or group in San Francisco can easily exploit cyber vulnerabilities in systems in New York, San Jose, Singapore, or wherever. This aspect of the cyber security problem is perhaps the most insidious, because the corresponding threat becomes more invisible and efficient than any other security threat in history.

Understanding Hacking

Many citizens – especially in the media – equate cyber security with hacking. Furthermore, most people have come to view hackers as some sort of computer terrorists, a perspective that has been more prevalent in the past few years. This is unfortunate, because it is simply not true. In fact, the expert hacking base in most countries is a potentially powerful ally in any fight against real cyber terrorism. Of course, by referring to hackers as terrorists, we alienate them from any national security goals.

It is worth pointing out that post-9/11 legislation in the United States, such as the Patriot Act, hasn't helped to clarify the distinction between hacking and terrorists. Editorials in publications ranging from hometown newspapers to *2600: The Hacker Quarterly*, have expressed serious concern about how such legislation broadened the definition of terrorism."[2]

---

[1] Oddly, if your television set crashed, you would take it back to the store and complain vociferously.

[2] *2600: The Hacker Quarterly* is published four times per year and devoted to hacking interests. The articles are excellent, and you can buy it at your local bookstore – using cash, dark glasses, and a phony name (just kidding).

Let's take a moment to explain what hacking is truly about, and why it has virtually nothing to do with terrorism. Perhaps the best illustration of the original concept of hacking, and what it really means, originated nearly three decades ago in one tiny hallway at AT&T Bell Laboratories in Murray Hill, New Jersey. The geniuses with offices in this hallway, *hackers*, as they were called at the time, were the inventors and programmers who created what you now know as the Unix operating system.

Their names – Ritchie, Kernighan, Morris, and Thompson – roll off the computer scientist's tongue like the names of Yankee hall-of-famers. They wore scraggly beards and sandals, and they stayed up half the night writing programs in the raw, native machine language of the computer. They were called hackers because they understood computer technology better than anyone else. The essence of hacking in those days was all about understanding computer technology. It involved having the ability to rip things apart and put them back together again.

Of course, these great Bell Labs hackers would never dream of breaking into computer systems that didn't belong to them. They also would never, ever consider intruding upon someone else's network for the purpose of stealing or destroying information. This sort of thing had nothing to do with understanding technology and it had nothing to do with hacking. It still doesn't.

Along these lines, I remember having a technical discussion in the mid-1980's with an experienced colleague of mine at Bell Labs. I didn't understand how one of the network protocol utilities functioned on a security system we were building for a government client. He agreed to offer some advice.

"There's only one sure way to learn how this thing works, Ed," he told me. "Only one way."

"What's that?"

"You've got to break it and then put it back together," he said. "That's the only way to understand it. You've got to hack it."

"I need to hack?"

"Yes."

So I hacked.

This was not cyber terrorism. It was hacking.

More recently, as youngsters have tried to emulate this spirit of learning through exploration, much of the original concept of hacking has been lost. The concept of hacking has morphed in some cases from the noble pursuit of technical understanding, into the less noble pursuit of mischievous vandalism. This is a terrible shame.

Misunderstanding the differences between hacking and cyber terrorism is also unfortunate, because hacking in its purest form plays an important role in the development of technology. We need technology experts to rip apart the various cyber systems that exist in our global infrastructure. Finding flaws in these systems should be considered a vital and noble act, one that enhances the security of any given nation. Sadly, this is not the case.

Hacking as a mischievous expression of youth can be traced directly to the early writings of Abbie Hoffman. His classic 1971 work, *Steal This Book*, provides an early glimpse into some of the more marginal activities commonly associated with hacking. I remember Hoffman's book being passed around the school bus when I was in grade school. One of his exploits involved taping a brick to a postcard that guaranteed return postage. "The company is required by law to pay this postage," Hoffman wrote. "You can also get rid of your garbage this way."

Why, you might ask, would anyone do such a thing? The answer is unclear, but Hoffman described ripping off big companies as an "act of communal love." This statement seems to me somewhat akin to the foolishness of youth, like the graffiti artist defacing a concrete overpass. Sure, when such acts have more sinister motivation such as extortion or theft, they represent crimes that must be dealt with harshly by law enforcement. But this is the minority of what hacking can and should be about.

True hackers sincerely believe they do the world a favor by exposing vulnerabilities. Consider the following fable: A village exists where everyone is so trusting that doors remain unlocked and valuables are left in the open. One day, a stranger moves in and notices these vulnerabilities. To demonstrate his observation, he breaks into everyone's homes, leaving notes explaining how easy it was to get in. When villagers see what has happened, they no longer trust each other, doors are locked, and valuables are now hidden in locked drawers.

The basic question of the story is this: Did the stranger do the villagers a disservice? Or did the stranger actually do them a favor? Keep in mind that nothing was stolen. The little caper was designed instead to expose vulnerabilities in the village. Perhaps someone from New Jersey might have moved into the town at a later date and really tried something truly awful. Everyone would have been grateful that they had been forewarned.

This fable nicely illustrates the *Consumer Reports*-type position of most hackers. They claim that by showing the world all the security vulnerabilities that exist in software and computers, they help us avert more serious problems, perhaps at the hands of cyber terrorists. They also claim that without their efforts, no one anywhere would be performing this vital service.

I must admit to being sympathetic to this claim. Certainly when hacking techniques are used for criminal purposes, no one condones such behavior, and law enforcement is required. We all know that hackers do, on occasion, break into places where they have no right to go. In these cases, they deserve strong punishments.

But when hacking is used to expose serious problems that must be fixed in critical infrastructure, that is arguably more good than bad for our society. Furthermore, every time a small, but largely impotent worm or virus hits the infrastructure, I can't help but wonder – and I know this is controversial – if this doesn't serve to keep us on our toes for the *big one*.

Information Warfare

The oft-mentioned concept of information warfare involves the use of computer and network hacking techniques between deliberate combatants in a time of war. Some people actually think this is how wars will be fought in the future. ("Ready ... aim ... hack!")

While it is a stretch to believe that hacking could replace the traditional battlefield, it is not hard to imagine computer and network attack techniques complementing existing warfare strategies and tactics. In fact, this situation already exists for virtually every military in the world. In these military environments, the complementary concept of information assurance involves armies using cyber security practices to counter information warfare. Many in government circles refer to information warfare as the offense, and information assurance as the defense.

In an essay called "From Scorched Earth to Information Warfare," Thomas Rona from the National Defense University explains how traditional warfare has often involved the devastation of an enemy countryside. This is done, he explains, with little regard for the cruel suffering that might be inflicted on local populations. "It became the preferred choice of military strategists," he writes, "not otherwise equipped to resist the momentum of heavily armored cavalry."

As you might guess, Rona points to the similarity between burning the cornfields, and the more current information warfare threat: "The modern version of the scorched earth principle," he warns, "becomes logically the destruction, incapacitation, and corruption of the enemy's information infrastructure."

The analogy is certainly reasonable. Security experts in the United States, for example, often lament that enemies would cause more suffering by shutting down television programming, than by distant military action. This would be relatively simple to do in many areas, since service providers have sprung up in recent years with dubious financials, weak operational models, and absolutely no attention to the cyber security threat. (You all know who you are.)

Interestingly, China, Taiwan, North Korea, South Korea, Japan, and Singapore have publicly acknowledged establishment of cyber warfare capabilities. Taiwan, in particular, has established a sizeable capability with several hundred troops. At one point, the Taiwanese even boasted that they had over a thousand potent viruses ready to be unleashed into China in the event of war. Gulp.[3]

Think for a moment about how recent and relatively benign viruses and worms such as Blaster, Sasser, and Mytob caused such havoc around the globe. Imagine a thousand more lethal worms being unleashed at once across our global infrastructure. Imagine further if these worms were designed to enter into corporate networks with the intent to seek and destroy important system files. The consequences to military systems, as well as civilian and business non-combatants would be horrific – especially since hardly anyone bothers to properly back up important files.

The United States military has apparently mobilized its own groups to take proactive steps to deal with the problem. The Air Force Information Warfare Center in San Antonio, for example, has assembled a world-class team of experts focused on prevention, detection, and response to military cyber attacks. This should not be surprising, given the long-standing goal in America to maintain military excellence in all relevant areas of warfare and protection.

Cyber Attacks Against Citizens

If you use a commercial operating system or software application (and who does not?), then you are probably familiar with the notion of a software patch. This is a small snippet of software that you get

---

[3] OK, I know I promised to leave the footnotes out, but in the interest of saving space in my email in-box, I pulled this claim from *The Next War Zone* by James Dunnigan (Citadel Press, 2002 – ISBN 0-8065-2413-8).

from your software manufacturer. It is designed to remove some vulnerability that hackers or cyber terrorists might exploit remotely. Think of it as duct tape for broken software.

If you do not patch your computer, and you connect it to the Internet, then your unpatched system will be discovered by software called a scanner. The scan operator – maybe a terrorist, maybe a twelve-year-old, maybe a thief – might then use this information to try to take advantage of your negligence. One of the ways this can be accomplished is to drop so-called zombie code into your machine. This zombie code will turn your system into an attack machine – probably without you even knowing it.[4]

Maybe you don't care that this vulnerability exists in your computer. Let's face it, as long as you can send and receive email, browse the Internet, and play games, what do you care if your computer is leading a life of crime? You might care if *you* were the target, but it's fair to presume that you might not blink otherwise.

Being the target of an attack comes in various flavors. The type of attack described above using zombies is generally designed to shut down some system, maybe a Web site. But there are other attacks that can have a more serious impact. Identity theft, in particular, has become a common problem on the Internet. Popular means to steal identities include something called *phishing*, in which phony emails are sent to unsuspecting users requesting personal data. If such an email is sent to one hundred thousand targets and ninety-nine percent ignore the request, then the attacker still obtains useful data from no less than a thousand individuals.

Other well-known techniques for computer attack include the use of spyware and viruses to steal information or cause some sort of trouble. Both are examples of software designed to run on your computer system in an unauthorized manner. Spyware tries to see what you are up to (such as your Web browsing interests), whereas

---

[4] Later, we'll explain this process, known as a distributed denial of service attack, in more detail. For now, imagine this attack as hiding missile launchers in your neighbors' garages.

viruses are often more malicious. In the worst case, a virus might try to delete files or corrupt your system.

The bottom line for users of computers is that these nagging cyber attack issues threaten the usefulness of the Internet. They also threaten the use of cyber systems in business and government, a situation that could have a negative impact on the global economy if we are not more careful.

Low Cost, High Return

You may have heard certain experts refer to the asymmetric nature of terrorism. This means that terrorists can generally cause large amounts of serious damage at very low cost. Think of this as a "mouse-that-roared" effect for computers.

Such asymmetry in terrorism is especially true in its cyber form. In the most extreme cases, individuals with little more than an Internet connected computer can produce substantial damage. In the majority of such cases, the most powerful weapon appears to be persistence. This goes not just for the cyber terrorist, but also for any malicious act using a computer and network, including cyber warfare and criminal attacks against citizens.

David Freedman and Charles Mann write of just such a cyber security case in their 1997 book, *At Large*. The book chronicles the exploits of a largely unskilled and untrained youngster using the moniker phantomd. This youth managed to insert so-called computer sniffer programs (think surveillance cameras) onto the Internet backbone. He had little experience, but simply refused to give up.

"Time after time, phantomd tried to log on," write Freedman and Mann, "and time after time he was rejected. He kept returning, believing that it was impossible for busy sysadmins to be careful 100 percent of the time. And eventually he got in."

This young man's persistence was so extraordinary that law enforcement watched in amazement while monitoring his computer keystrokes. There he was, typing away into the early hours of morning. Then suddenly, the government surveillance teams would watch as a constant stream of single digits would flow from the keyboard. Their subject, they soon realized, had fallen asleep, face first onto the keyboard ("zzzzz"). Then, sure enough, after a brief period of dozing, he would wake up rejuvenated, and would begin going at it again.

Such determination generally results in success, and we must presume that any terrorists would be just as stubborn. To test this, many corporations employ computer security specialists to simulate cyber attacks on their infrastructure. These experts are organized into tiger teams that require little more than a few computers with network connections. They design attacks on their own systems to identify soft spots. In over two decades, I've never seen a tiger team *not* get into something interesting during a penetration test.

You may also be surprised to know that the types of tools required to commit acts of cyber terror are often available for free on the Internet. The Chief Information Officer of a large government agency in Washington was once in our network security laboratory at AT&T and asked me about this.

"Can you really download free attack tools from the Internet?" she asked. "That sounds more dangerous than I'd ever be comfortable with."

Being somewhat mischievous, I pointed over to the two security engineers from her agency who had just heard their boss's question and who were now trying to hide.

"Well?" she asked, turning to them. "Do you guys have an opinion on this? Surely we wouldn't use such tools, would we?"

One of them cleared his throat.

"We, uh," he stammered hesitantly, "we were just telling Ed that, uh, we use these freeware attack tools downloaded from the Internet just about every day."

So if these attack tools are good enough for use in government applications, then you can be certain that they are good enough for cyber terrorists and criminals. The most frightening aspect of the whole situation is that such tools remove the difficulty factor in cyber attack. You simply download, install, point, and click.[5]

The resulting damage that can be caused by cyber terrorists armed with nothing more than free attack tools is staggering. The distributed denial of service or DDOS attack, for example, works in this manner. Vulnerabilities are reported or found, exploits are developed, and eventually some freely downloadable tool emerges. Don't be deluded into thinking that the resultant attack is any less lethal because it's launched using such a free tool.

Our security team at AT&T, for instance, first encountered truly effective downloadable DDOS attack tools in the summer of 1999. During that time, we had been entrusted with the security design, operation, and protection of the White House's Y2K Information Coordination Center (ICC) in Washington. Obviously, we became paranoid that this type of attack would happen to us. After all, the Y2K ICC would be set up to run for only a couple of days before and after the Millennium change – a perfect period of time for a terrorist to bring our site down.

Our cyber security design lead at the time, Steve Schuster (he's now head of cyber security at Cornell University), initiated a crusade with senior management to make certain that every possible step was taken to address this attack. We researched and simulated DDOS attacks on test beds – to frightening results, and we brought in experts from AT&T Labs Research to help us prepare. Quite a few rolls of Tums were consumed during that time, because we all realized just how problematic this attack could be.

We ended up installing redundant, diverse security systems with world-class experts seated behind the consoles, and we took the time to spin up senior officials on this denial of service threat. This included everyone from our corporate officers in AT&T to senior government officials, including the President. ("So tell me again,

---

[5] Later in the book, we'll examine how law enforcement might use deception to mitigate the risk of hacking tool downloads.

guys," we would hear from snickering officials with lofty titles. "You're saying that some kid can shut down our ICC with a PC?")

Happily, nothing much happened. I remember our team being ribbed somewhat by colleagues in the days and weeks that followed. The joking stopped, of course, several months later when CNN, eBay, Yahoo, and other popular Internet e-commerce sites were shut down by a distributed denial of service attack, pretty much along the lines that we had envisioned and explained. (And no, we did not do it.)

National Cyber Dependence

Cyber terrorism is obviously less frightening than planes slamming into buildings or suicide bombers blowing themselves up in crowded malls. Cyber terrorism is also considerably less intense than nuclear, biological, and chemical attacks. Furthermore, the idea of hackers defacing Web sites or reporting buffer overflow errors in some software seems more a nuisance than something that businesses and government should be seriously concerned with.

A few years ago, Lawrence Kudlow, the popular economist and television talk show host, asked me a question along the same lines.

"So the Internet goes down and some kids can't surf the net for a few hours," he joked over a breakfast meeting in Manhattan. "Who cares?"

Well, in one sense, he's right. The Internet going down for a few hours is certainly serious, but it is obviously not in the same category as an NBC attack. No one could reasonably dispute that claim. No one. But we must be careful.

The critical infrastructure components of most nations are dependent on computers and networks. To the degree that terrorists gain access to these computers and networks, they may also be capable of seriously disrupting or even remotely controlling these services. This includes nuclear and conventional power plants, transportation systems, telecommunications services, emergency services, government infrastructure, and water supplies.

The consequences of this can be stated rather succinctly as follows: If a nation is dependent on critical infrastructure elements, then it is also dependent on their underlying computer and network systems. In fact, this is an important enough central theme, that it deserves to be highlighted in the context of an attack strategy on critical infrastructure components:

An effective way to attack critical infrastructure is to target the underlying software, computers, and networks.

People can certainly view cyber attack as passé compared to hijacking, or bombs, or chemical attacks. They can joke that losing Internet access might improve your productivity at work. They can further joke (like my wife) that having all the computers and Blackberry devices in the world down for a while might produce some needed quiet, rest, and relaxation.

But no one can dispute the implications of cyber attack on critical infrastructure. Emergency services, transportation systems, telecommunications, and the like, have evolved from humble beginnings into complex automated infrastructure that cannot operate properly without software, computers, and networks. As such, they can be attacked more readily.

This evolution can be illustrated in the context of a simple grocery store. In the old days, the grocer hopped into a pick-up truck, drove to the local farm market, loaded up some boxes with fresh veggies, and brought them back to the store. A stock boy would unload the boxes and put the veggies out on the shelves for sale. Even with computers the size of tractors, hackers could not disrupt this simple process.

Modern grocers follow a different process today. Computer systems monitor inventories and interact over networks with suppliers in real-time. Stock rooms hold only the minimum of what is needed, because the supply chain has become so efficient. While it might be a bit of a stretch to imagine cyber terrorists going after your local Piggly Wiggly supermarket, the attack likelihood is certainly there for more serious infrastructure components.

Poor Security Practices

The cyber security practices of government, business, and citizens have been uniformly abysmal. This is true in virtually every sector of every country around the world. We should be ashamed of ourselves.

Poorly set up computer systems with vulnerable and broken software, located on networks with unabated access from the outside, are so prevalent across the globe, that the word *epidemic* comes to mind. The situation is not unlike the bad eating, drinking, and smoking habits one sees in so many countries: People know better, but they do it anyway.

"Many, many companies and government agencies are still pursuing security strategies as if we were back in the mainframes era of 1975," writes software guru Edward Yourdon in his book, *Byte Wars*. "Not only that, we're now living in a world with literally millions of powerful personal computers with high-speed, always-on cable/DSL connections to the Internet, owned and operated by technologically naïve consumers."

Roughly speaking, poor cyber security practices fall into the following three categories:

- Software Practices: This involves poor processes leading to vulnerable code.
- System Administrative Practices: This involves inadequate administrative processes for applications, computers, networks, or other infrastructure components.
- Security Practices: This involves improper selection, configuration, integration, or use of explicit cyber security protections.

Blame poor software practice on software manufacturers and distributors. Their processes should be more robust, and their products should not be so buggy. Blame the other two categories on the people running the computer and network systems – they are often not doing their jobs properly. (Actually, in many cases, you should blame all the stingy managers who refuse to fund proper security and system administrative initiatives.)

Poor cyber security practices are also complemented by deficiencies in other aspects of system security. Physical security, for example, is often done poorly in an enterprise. Bad physical security allows cyber terrorists to combine their remote attacks with more tangible access to facility-based resources. In addition, poor physical security often makes it difficult to diagnose the real origin of a given problem.

As an illustration, several years ago, a major bank in London asked our security group at AT&T to help them deal with desktop PCs that were being stolen from their branch offices in England. Apparently, the theft was becoming rather prevalent, and it was causing quite a stir, especially with the bank's privacy team.

The bank initiated the discussion with our engineers by suggesting that we should simply encrypt the PC disks. With the disks encrypted, they reasoned, the computer thieves would examine the stolen machines only to discover that no vital customer financial information would be available. As long as the encryption routines were difficult to break, it was further argued, no cryptanalytic attack would work either. The attack would thus be thwarted by the use of encryption, or so it was explained to us.

So we concentrated and created some sort of encryption solution, until someone from our team was bold enough to ask the following question: Didn't the bank think it a bit unacceptable that computers were being stolen from branch offices? Perhaps, we suggested, some improvements in physical security might be a better investment than encryption.[6]

In addition to poor physical security, incredibly lax personnel security practices abound in many corporate and government organizations, especially in America. State-of-the-art personnel security programs presume that previous behavior is a good predictor of future behavior. Thus, if you've been a bad person in the past, then the theory is that you'll probably continue to be a bad person in the future.

This presumption may be correct, but some people have managed to reform themselves from past lives. An example is Frank Abagnale, author of the well-known book (and Spielberg movie) *Catch Me If You Can*. Abagnale spent the better part of his youth defrauding airlines and other institutions, and he's now a trusted security consultant to groups like the FBI.

"I'm still a con artist," he jokes in his recent book, *The Art of the Steal*. "I'm just putting down a positive con these days as opposed to the negative con I used in the past. I've merely redirected the talents I've always possessed. I've applied the same relentless attention to working on stopping fraud that I once applied to perpetuating fraud."

A final type of security worth mentioning is known in government circles as operations security. This generally involves careful planning and execution to ensure that some operational maneuver will be secure. As an example, consider that when government dignitaries come to town, one finds the inevitable entourage of earpiece-wearing bodyguards. They always seem to be talking on their radios and skittering around looking suspiciously at everything that moves. This, of course, is the operations security team.

---

[6] We did find out that banking regulations were at play, and that external auditors were requiring the encryption. Nevertheless, the systems should not have been so easily lifted out of branch offices.

To illustrate the skills required to be good at operations security, I often pose the following puzzle to audiences and graduate students: Suppose that you had an elephant named Bob and you needed to parade Bob down Fifth Avenue in Manhattan without anyone at all noticing him. How would you do this?

Some students suggest throwing a big blanket over Bob. Others suggest putting him in a big tractor. Still others suggest various forms of camouflage for the elephant. Of course, those with the most promise as future operations security experts offer the best solution: Simply parade Bob down Fifth Avenue in a herd of other elephants.

Bugs in Our Software

As suggested above, the software powering our computer and network systems is shamefully broken. No computer security or software expert denies this fact. It is common knowledge, and yet, it is rarely discussed – and I'm not sure why.

The fact that we say our software is broken does not mean that it is broken beyond acceptable day-to-day usage, because that would cause a global uprising. The situation instead is that most software, whether it's purchased off-the-shelf or custom designed by a software firm, usually works pretty well, but has a lot of bugs that might or might not be found. When they are found, they sometimes can be exploited to cause serious malicious damage.

To understand the absurd security situation we have in our software, let's consider a simple non-computing analogy. Suppose that you have just purchased a new car, and you realize that your new car has a serious flaw. Maybe the roof of the car flies off when you depress the brake while turning the wheel to the left with the blinker on – or something completely ludicrous like that.

Think for a moment about how you would feel if this were to happen to you. You would want to know why the car hadn't been tested properly. You would want to know why quality initiatives weren't in place to prevent such a thing from occurring. You would want to know how such a serious flaw could go unnoticed through the design and manufacturing process. You would write letters to your local newspaper. You would probably want to sue the car company.

"Automobiles are manufactured by the millions," writes Professor Henry Petroski from Duke University, "but it would not do to have them failing with a snap on the highways the way light bulbs and shoelaces do."

Unfortunately, car owners know that this sort of thing does occasionally happen. Not often, but it does happen. Do you remember Jacques Nasser, former CEO of Ford, apologizing several years ago on television for the recall of defective Firestone tires on his vehicles? According to CBS News at the time, the whole mess cost Ford and Firestone three billion dollars. It was not a pretty thing to watch.

In contrast, no software executive has ever gone on television to apologize for a design or manufacturing flaw. This is not because the effects of such problems are insignificant. Consider this: A Viking spacecraft once went hurtling into space as a result of a programming error. A military aircraft with poorly written software flipped upside-down in mid-flight when it crossed the Equator. (OK, OK – it was only the flight simulator that did the flipping, but this is still frightening.)

Here are some more: Massive doses of radiation injured or killed six people over a two-year period as a result of software flaws. Even the operating system software used during the writing of this book crashed several times, once so catastrophically that several pages of writing were lost. ("This sort of thing happens all the time with software," I was told by the PC support staff at AT&T.)

Consider the following additional disaster scenario from Professor Petroski which might ruin tonight's sleep for you: "An incident with a nuclear power plant piping program occurred several years ago," he wrote recently. "An incorrect sign was discovered in one of the instructions to the computer. Stresses that should have been added were subtracted." Yikes.

Here is the most important point: If software bugs were nothing more than a nuisance that could be dealt with via patching, then there would be no big deal. But since these software bugs can be remotely exploited by malicious individuals and groups, it truly is a big deal.

Amateur Construction of Software

You may be surprised to know that non-engineering professionals created your software. I can state this, because no generally recognized standards exist for what constitutes a professional software engineer. This doesn't mean that there aren't smart people developing software. It means, rather, that their profession exists in an era that will eventually be viewed as the Stone Ages of software.

In the software industry today, pretty much anyone with a computer can write code, and the result is a lot of buggy, vulnerable software. Sure, there are many, many skilled and professional programmers with great training and advanced degrees. I've been a professor of computer science at the Stevens Institute of Technology for seventeen years and have helped to train software professionals myself. Furthermore, much excellent software does exist in all walks and circles. But the truth is that for the most part, the software industry has hardly been a pillar of engineering professionalism.

By way of contrast, the more mature branches of engineering have carefully crafted sets of standards and certifications that define what it means to be a professional engineer. Examinations for professional engineers, for instance, are tough to pass and require significant formal background and training. There is no notion, for example, of someone just "taking up" civil engineering because it looks like fun. Software engineers, however, seem to pop up all the time with little more training than a couple of books and some general interest.

One incident that illustrates this point occurred back in the late nineties, when I was asked to give a talk on computer and network security at a World Wide Web conference in New York. After my talk, I was standing near the refreshment table and accidentally knocked over a cup of grape juice. To my horror, the juice spilled all over the table and down onto the white slacks of a woman standing nearby.

I rushed around looking for some napkins or a washcloth or anything that might help the situation. But we both realized there wasn't much I could do – I'd ruined her pants. Feeling somewhat guilty, I tried to make pleasant conversation. Her conference badge said that she was the Founder and CEO of a software company with a long and impressive sounding name. I don't remember the exact name, but it was something like this: National Web-Based Software for Safety and Mission-Critical Applications. Or whatever.

"That's some company name," I said. "What do you do?"

She replied with a perfect little marketing speech:

"Our company," she explained, "was founded to provide critical Internet software and complex engineering solutions for Web-based safety and mission-critical infrastructure applications."

I was impressed.

"So tell me," I asked, "what's your background? Computer science? Electrical engineering?"

She smiled and shook her head.

"Oh, no," she replied. "I was an English major in college. I used to write poetry, but it just didn't make enough to pay the bills. So I went into software."

Now you should know that I have absolutely nothing against poets. But if you told me that the Tappan Zee Bridge was designed by a person with an English major who writes poetry and has no engineering background, then I would stay out of Tarrytown.

Three Futures for Cyber Security

My observation is that our globe is currently at an important crossroads in the area of cyber security. This crossroads appears to have three possible futures – each of equal likelihood. Unfortunately, the consequences of each path are anything but equal. Let's examine each one in turn.

Path 1: Continued Uncertainty

The first path involves continued uncertainty about everything cyber security-related. This continued uncertainty would stem from the same sort of ignorance and naiveté that I think exists in most circles around real cyber security risks. This path also has the unfortunate side effect of continuing our present inability to accurately quantify or even qualify the cyber security posture of any nation.

To illustrate this level of continued uncertainty, consider that Chief Information Security Officers can rarely explain how they would deal with an announced cyber security threat to their systems. I ask them what they would do if they received credible information that someone was going to hit their systems at a specified time. The responses are frighteningly weak.

I've heard some state that they would go into a so-called heightened state of alert. I've heard some state that they would try to look at their systems for anything funny – whatever in the world that means. I've seen some respond by simply shrugging, saying that the scenario could never happen. I've even seen some respond with a straight face that they would call the local police.

This casual and confused approach to cyber security is utterly insufficient in the face of expert cyber terrorists who can dance around most types of security protections. National infrastructure requires a more professional and rigorous treatment, especially in the face of aggressive and capable terrorist adversaries. So this first future scenario path involving more-of-the-same is therefore unacceptable because ignorance and luck are simply not sufficient to keep us safe.

Path 2: Digital Pearl Harbor

The second cyber security path has much worse consequences. This is the so-called Digital Pearl Harbor scenario. It involves future collapse of critical computer and network infrastructure as a result of some diabolically planned terrorist attack that exploits vulnerabilities in global critical infrastructure. My belief is that this future path is as likely as the others, a view that produces some disagreement among experts.

"The sky hasn't fallen yet, but it soon may," writes technology expert Simson Garfinkel in a recent essay. He goes on to acknowledge the on-going debate between those who believe a cyber catastrophe might occur and the simple fact that it has not yet happened. "Why," he asks, "didn't Iraqi military start attacking us in cyber space when we started bombing their country?" No one has a good answer, but the potential for such action grows every day.

Some sources in the United States government attribute the lack of retaliation by cyber terrorists to improvements that have occurred in our computer security. It is true that security managers across the United States have done a better job in recent years of ensuring that security policies are in place (sometimes), that better forms of authentication are used (most of the time), and that lines of communication have been created between response centers (even though it's not always clear what information can or should be shared).

But any suggestion that we've averted cyber retaliation through coordinated security improvements is far-fetched. This view violates one of the most basic tenets of cyber security:

During a period of seeming quiet, never confuse good luck with improved cyber security.

In fact, other than more efficient patching, no evidence of any substantive cyber security improvements exists in any country, and terrorist sleeper cells could easily include members with computer science degrees. It is therefore reasonable to presume that a Digital Pearl Harbor against some national target could occur at any time in the near future, unless something specific is done to reduce this risk.

Path 3: Enlightened Global Security

The third possible path for cyber security is the most desirable. It is a bright future in which cyber infrastructure security risk is greatly diminished. It is a future as divorced from current national infrastructure security approach as, say, our current system of air travel is from the days of the Wright brothers. But it is a future that will require dramatic changes and investments in our infrastructure security approaches.

The ensuing pages detail the issues that must be understood by citizens, managers, and technologists for us to reach this third global cyber security vision. Hopefully, it will help inspire citizens and leaders to consider a different and more enlightened course of action in the way software, computers, and networks are used, protected, and depended upon in critical infrastructure.

2 Understanding Cyber Attacks

A DECADE OR SO AGO, I was invited to teach a network security class to a group of technologists in Washington. After a day or so of lecturing, I was approached during one of the breaks by two of the participants:

"This is very helpful," one participant commented, "but we're wondering if you could help us with a couple of these acronyms."

"A couple of the acronyms?"

"Yes. We're a bit lost."

I gulped. The participants were in charge of computer and network security implementation, and were advertised as mostly system administrators and engineers. I'd just spent the past two hours explaining the intricate details of various Internet attacks. I'd assumed that this material was a review for these people.

"Which acronyms are you having trouble with?"

"Let's see, uh, ... first of all, what do you mean by that one acronym you keep using."

I gulped again. I had explicitly avoided using obscure references.

"Which acronym?" I asked.

"Uh, let's see. We're not sure what you mean by ... IP."

(For readers who might not get the point: IP stands for Internet Protocol. Anyone who is of a technical mindset and works with computers should know exactly what this stands for.)

During that period of my career in the early 1990's, I was traveling around the world explaining how security problems in the Internet Protocol suite and the Unix operating system were placing us all at risk. My talks were well received, but it never occurred to me at the time that listeners – even those with technical backgrounds – might not understand what in the world I was trying to explain.

The question about "IP" from these two seminar participants left a deep impression on me. I soon came to the conclusion that the best way to explain cyber attack to a general, non-technical audience was through the use of non-computing analogies. These analogies could be used to extract basic principles in an obvious manner, without scaring listeners with the details of a given underlying computing technology.

One must be careful with analogies, however, because they can take on a life of their own. Computer viruses, for example, are often described in terms of biological viruses. It turns out that this analogy just doesn't work for computer viruses beyond the most superficial level. It breaks down rather quickly when you get into the details of how computers actually work. So again: One must be very, very careful with analogies.

That said, let us start our discussion on the basics of cyber attack with our first simple analogy: Safecracking.

Feynmann's Safecracking

Professor Richard Feynmann, the Nobel Prize winning physicist, recounts in his popular book, *Surely You're Joking, Mr. Feynmann,* how he learned to crack safes during the (ahem) Manhattan Project. His techniques have important implications for cyber security today.

His greatest exploit involved breaking into the personal safes of Frederic de Hoffman just after World War II. These safes contained the secrets necessary to construct the atomic bomb, including procedures for generating neutrons and schedules for producing plutonium. Feynmann joked later that this massive payload makes him the greatest safecracker of all time. "I opened safes whose contents were bigger and more valuable that what any safecracker had opened," jibed Feynmann. "I have them all beat!"

Amazingly, he broke into these safes by simply guessing that de Hoffman would use a mathematical constant as his combination. He started by trying $pi = 3.14159$ as the combination. No luck. Then he tried the base of natural logarithms $e = 2.71828$, perhaps the second most important constant used by physicists. Sure enough – click – each of de Hoffman's safes opened with the combination 27-18-28. In some sense, this is the physicist's equivalent of using one's birth date or phone number as a computer system password.

Now, let's pause for a test: Do you use digits from your phone number as a PIN for your ATM card? If so, then don't lose the card, because your phone number can be looked up from the name on the card. You may wish to set this book down for a moment to go change your PIN.

Back to safecracking: Feynmann also managed to open the safes of his associates by noticing an interesting fact. When the drawers of the safes were left open, anyone could fiddle with the dial, rotating it back and forth – just *so* – to find the first two of the combination numbers. "I'd just wobble the dial back and forth, back and forth," he explained. "When I got back to my office, I would write the two numbers down on a piece of paper."

It apparently required some practice to feel the click as the dial rotated, but Feynmann easily mastered the technique. He would casually perform this fiddling while visiting the offices of colleagues. Over time, he pretty much had everyone's combination. Most of the scientists working with Feynmann were totally oblivious to this attack, and had no idea that anyone was exploiting their presumed security.

As you might guess, there was an easy way to beat this attack: The owner simply had to keep his safe closed when not in use! What was needed was proper configuration and usage of the safe – something we would call system administration in computing today. When Feynmann explained to a senior military officer the need for everyone to keep their safes closed when others were present, the suggestion went virtually ignored. Instead, people decided that the best security technique was to simply keep Richard Feynmann out of their offices!

This irrational knee-jerk reaction happens to present-day hackers all the time. They find an exploit, expose it, and are accused of being the problem. This is like blaming a *Consumer Reports* article for the brake lining weakness it exposes. Sure, hacking techniques, unlike brake lining problems, can be exploited remotely by terrorists. As a result, more care must be exercised in trouble reporting. But this shoot-the-messenger approach diverts security responsibility away from the creators and users of technology toward anyone brave enough to expose the problem.

By the way, a rational argument can also be made that the real bad guys – terrorists who are stockpiling attack information – already know about most security problems. As a result, when hackers publicly expose some cyber vulnerability, we might interpret this as defusing a cyber attack weapon already in the possession of a terrorist. How is that for a paradigm shift in the way we view hackers?

Back to Feynmann: He writes in his book of a basement technician working at Los Alamos with a reputation for also being an expert at breaking into safes. After some investigation, Feynmann meets the technician and soon learns that this man's technique involved using the manufacturer's default combination to open big safes. Apparently the defaults worked for one in every five safes he tried in and around Los Alamos.

The implications here are staggering. These famous scientists, even though they were dealing with *nuclear secrets*, were either too lazy or too ignorant to change the initial setting on their safes. Of course, such laziness with default settings continues in computing today. How many computer and network administrators and users never bother to change their default password? How many are just as lazy in their selection of passwords, even if the consequences of break-in are severe? The answer is almost everyone.

Here is a simple personal illustration: Several years ago, during a food court lunch at the Livingston Mall in New Jersey, a sales colleague asked if I could break into the computers sitting on the sales display shelves at one of the mall's department stores. "You're supposed to be Mr. Security," he joked, as we finished our lunch. "Let's see how good you really are."

I tried to come up some excuse, because I didn't think I could do it. To be honest, I'm really not much of a hacker. But then I remembered reading in *2600 Magazine* that many of the Apple personal computers being shipped to retail stores at the time were loaded with the default password of 'familymacintosh'.

The question was thus whether the sales demo program running on the Apple computers in this mall would have this password. We finished our pizza and walked over to the store. We approached the keyboard of an Apple PC, and I used the standard three-finger Apple escape to quit the demo program. We watched as the password box popped up. I then tried the default password, and – *ta da*! – it worked perfectly. We had by-passed the demo program and now pretty much owned the machine.

By the way, in case you're wondering, we called the salesperson over and demonstrated this security problem to him. He was not amused, and even appeared ready to call Mall Security. Figuring that this might not be the most career enhancing moment for either of us, we got out of there quickly.

The key cyber security learning from Richard Feynmann is that the simplest methods are often all that is needed to break into a computer or network system. Default passwords, easy to guess passwords, and poorly configured protection systems are the scourge of cyber security. Because we are all so sloppy, terrorists and criminals don't have to start with complex procedures requiring great skill. Our laziness is often more than enough to provide a wide open door to attack.

One frightening footnote to this discussion is that absolutely no evidence exists that passwords and their associated security practice are any better in critical infrastructure systems. In fact, it's been my unfortunate experience during two decades in this field working on a range of nationally critical computer and network systems that the general security practices found in such settings are not much better than one might find employed by a non-expert on a home computer.

Cracking an Old Soda Machine

You might remember that many soda vending machines during the Sixties and early Seventies had a narrow glass door on the front. You would open this glass door, pay your quarter, and pull a soda bottle out. Until you paid, however, the bottle would not come out, even though you could actually tug on the exposed bottle top. (If this Vintage Vendo design is not familiar to you, then we must not share a generation. Go ahead and Google the terms to see what one looks like.)

In any event, nasty kids like me figured out pretty quickly that if you carried a bottle opener in your pocket, you could pop the top off the bottle while it was still in the machine, and sip out all the soda with a straw. Some of the neater kids would open the top and just let the soda spill out into a paper cup that they would bring along for the occasion. It was an elegant attack and it worked every time.

There was a soda machine like this in front of a gun shop near my home on Route 35 along the New Jersey Shore. My cousins and I would hit this machine pretty regularly for free soft drinks in the summer. It's a classic instance of attackers targeting the valued payload (the soda) rather than the useless container (the bottle). In computing terms, it's like stealing the informational contents of a file rather than the file itself.

I tell this story frequently around the world, often asking audiences of all backgrounds and experience levels how they would fix this problem. I ask them to imagine that they are a candy shop owner with this type of soda machine outside the store. I ask them to share what they would do to solve the problem if local kids were stealing soda from their machine regularly.

Someone usually suggests flipping the bottles around in the machine. This works fine for cans, but soda bottles with the classic hourglass design can't be flipped around in this type of machine. Even if flipping the bottles around was possible, this would require a change in the procedure for loading the machine, known in computing parlance as a change in the way a system is administered. You'd have to convince the soda delivery guy to do this and you might get hassled, or charged more, or whatever.

Computer and software vendors also do not make life easy for secure system administration. Software is generally shipped in a configuration that requires explicit and often complex changes to make it properly secure. For example, if you buy software that contains optional features, your manufacturer will probably ship the software to you with these features enabled. This makes things easier for their help desk staff in the event that you need assistance using these features. But it also makes things easier for intruders trying to get into your system.

If, for security reasons, you want these features turned off, then you will almost always have to do it yourself. This process of turning off all unnecessary features on a computer system is known as security hardening. System administrators actually attend training courses on how to do this for operating systems like Unix and Windows. As such, the name of this process is quite appropriate: It is very *hard* to do.

Back to our soda machine: Another proposed fix involves the use of a surveillance camera. Certainly, if you hang a camera in a visible location near the machine, then you will scare many kids away. ("Hey, guys, look! There's a camera – let's get out of here!") This approach is similar to placing the warning sign for a home security system in your landscaping. In both cases, you're trying to prevent an attack by announcing that someone is watching.

Of course, attackers might not believe that anyone is actually watching. Alternatively, they might not even care (think of the evil terrorist waving to the camera while driving a truck bomb into a building complex). In such cases, cameras and signs are utterly irrelevant to security. An obvious implication is that while surveillance might work to stop some forms of hacking, it will probably not prove to be the most effective deterrent to cyber terrorism.

On the other hand, if you take a somewhat different approach and put a hidden camera in place, then you might actually catch someone in a malicious act. One must be careful with this strategy, however, because the camera watches along helplessly when an attack begins. Security measures can only be initiated after evidence of an attack can be seen. In addition, this approach won't scare anyone away, because the attacker won't know you are watching. In the computing and networking world, this process of surveillance is called intrusion detection.

Oddly, many companies in America have created the sad situation of installing intrusion detection systems that are hidden from the attacker and that include no infrastructure for watching or responding to the output. The result is nothing more than wasted time, money, and energy. Managers of businesses using this approach generally become frustrated that their security investments are not working. And they begin looking for alternate solutions.

An entire industry called the Managed Security Service Provider (MSSP) industry has emerged so that businesses might consider outsourcing this task. An MSSP generally advertises its services by depicting rows of intense operations staff sitting in front of monitors, carefully watching everything that is going on. The jury is still out on whether the MSSP outsourcing model truly works for most businesses. Obviously, it's better than just ignoring the surveillance output.

Let's return to our hacked soda machine: Yet another suggested fix involves placing a sign in front of the machine telling kids to quit stealing soda by popping the caps. This has the obvious and humorous effect of teaching the more ignorant kids about the details of the attack. ("Note to nasty kids: Please do not use a bottle opener to open the bottles and drink all the soda out!") Arguably, if such a sign were put on the face of your machine, you would see more, rather than less theft.

On the Internet, organizations like the Computer Emergency Response Team Coordination Center (CERT/CC) at Carnegie-Mellon University have to deal with just this sort of notification problem. They serve as cyber attack clearinghouses by providing information about security issues that might be brewing. As such, CERT and similar organizations try to issue useful alerts about problems without giving away too much information to existing or potential bad guys. Good luck.

From a cyber terrorist perspective, the implications of the soda machine attack and its potential fixes are profound. Specifically, the example demonstrates the management decoupling between the size of a security problem and the size of its associated security solution. Specifically, the problem arises that small security problems often require huge fixes – a non-robust situation that greatly complicates security planning and management.

To illustrate this point, consider that our vending machine problem was fixed by no less than a total redesign in the way these machines operate. This redesign came at great expense and inconvenience to the vending machine industry. This example should cause concern for operators of critical infrastructure for obvious reasons: In certain cases, seemingly small vulnerabilities in a nation's critical services might only be fixed by massive redesigns of infrastructure.

Consider the following example: hackers have been known to use simple software scripts called mail bombs. Such attack programs barrage a victim with tons of useless email, often by signing the victim up to receive email from many different mailing lists. The result of such forgery is that the victim's email address becomes flooded with garbage. It's an easy attack – one that requires zero skill to execute. "The ease with which one may forge perfect email," writes Carolyn Meinel in her book, *The Happy Hacker*, "may well be the greatest threat the Internet faces today."

Think for a moment about how you might try to solve this problem if it happened to you. Your first thought would be to try to cancel your forged membership in all of these mailing lists. Unfortunately, this is not an easy process because you would have to find all the lists to which you were joined. Then you'd have to cancel your membership, often by email – and we just agreed that your email was down!

So perhaps it is more likely that you would decide to simply change your email address. This is easy enough to do mechanically, but don't forget that you would also have to notify all of your friends, business associates, and valid lists to which you belong that your email address has changed. So this is obviously not a desirable process either.

It turns out that the general issue of protecting Internet mailing lists from forgery is only achieved through on-going changes in the design and protocol for how people sign up for such lists. This illustrates the effect of a seemingly small vulnerability causing huge problems.

Internet Worms

An Internet worm is a computer program that is designed to spread like wild fire across a network. Unlike a forest fire, however, a worm can spread to large numbers of computers almost instantaneously. Such rapid proliferation implies that human defenders seated behind computer consoles watching for attack patterns in some computerized animation will not stop worms. The attack will have come and gone before any human being could ever hope to have detected it and responded.

As you probably already know, Internet worms have become an unfortunate fact of life for system and network administrators across the globe. Many of these worms propagate by blasting themselves to a range of email addresses found in some user's compromised account. Several years ago, David Smith – a software development contractor working in my location at AT&T (gulp!) – was caught having unleashed a virus program called Melissa that worked roughly in this manner.

On January 25, 2003, an Internet worm called Slammer hit nearly 60,000 servers on the Internet, taking advantage of security vulnerabilities in Microsoft's SQL software. Companies scrambled to contain the worm inside local area networks and to patch their computers with the appropriate bug fixes. In those cases where the Microsoft patch was not performed, perhaps because it might have broken certain applications running on the server, the worm was successful in attacking the unpatched software.

Here's how an Internet worm works: First, the worm program finds some Internet-connected computer that it can communicate with. Second, it copies itself over the Internet onto that computer. Third, it remotely executes itself on that computer. That's it. Of course, a malicious designer would include additional nasty functionality to destroy files, guess passwords, or even crash applications. But it's not required.

What is required, however, is some procedure for the worm to self-propagate across the network. This self-propagation would be impossible in the absence of a common computing environment. That is, a worm program depends on its code being able to run across multiple machines, a requirement driven by the goals of software portability and interoperability. The overall profound effect can be stated as follows:

> *Interoperability and common computing environments make cyber attacks easier.*

Most computer scientists have chosen to conveniently ignore this basic, but obvious fact. Global network connectivity with interoperable applications like instant messaging, email, and interactive gaming enables collaboration, productivity, entertainment, new business opportunities, and fun. But the negative security consequences of this functionality cannot be ignored.

Consider, for example, the impressive Google Earth program. It flies you to any destination on Earth and offers a bird's eye visual view from above of your target destination. It's a reconnaissance junkie's dream. But the security and privacy implications of this powerful tool have barely been discussed. In a world where people have come to view IP addresses as private, how will they now feel about the ubiquity of visual access to their homes?

Likewise, the spread of ubiquitous computing in the coming years could be expected to exhibit security drawbacks. All sorts of interesting attack scenarios arise when your home heating system, DVD player, iPod, refrigerator, and watch all have Internet addresses for communications. God help us as this technology becomes more available to cyber attackers. Terrorist messages will begin popping up from worms that find their way into our two-year-olds' Sit'n'Spell games.

Internet Protocol Attacks

In order to illustrate how attacks exploit the use of protocols, let's recall the most familiar non-computing protocol we follow all day long: Talking on the telephone. You know how it works:

1. I pick up my phone and dial your number.

2. You hear the ring tone on your phone, and you answer it by pushing a button and then grunting some sort of greeting.[7]

---

[7] In the old days, you would actually be home to answer the phone and would say something like 'Jones Residence'. You never hear this anymore because no one is ever home and mobile phones are not bound to location.

3. After you grunt your initial greeting, I grunt something back and now our initial handshake is completed.

After these first three steps, we've identified each other, and we know who we are talking to based primarily on familiarity of voice and circumstance ("Hi, Mom, I was expecting your call"). Telemarketers claim neither advantage, so they try to trick us into completing the initial handshake by propping up their stated credentials.

4. Once we've finished chatting away together, we engage in a final handshake of mutual goodbye grunts and then we're done. We both hang up the phone and that's it.

As we all know, this is a mature protocol – one that is well understood and obviously useful in our everyday lives. There are millions of different twists on this protocol, such as when different languages are required, but for the most part, voice conversations by phone work pretty well.

Computers on the Internet, it turns out, communicate using a protocol that is surprisingly similar to the phone exchange we just dissected.

Step 1: One computer starts a conversation – usually called a session – with another computer over the Internet by sending it a randomly generated number. It finds the target computer by looking up its address – sort of like looking up a phone number. There is even a large yellow pages-like directory called the domain name system (DNS) that is intended to help with this lookup process.[8]

Step 2: The receiving computer responds to this initial message with an acknowledgment of the random number, and then provides a second randomly generated number (like grunting your greeting into the phone).

---

[8] Many experts view the domain name system as the biggest vulnerability on the Internet because of the ease with which one can pollute entries. Using this utility, attackers can blind out domain names on the Internet – and when this happens, it's not easy to fix.

Step 3: The original computer then acknowledges the second random number and the two machines have now completed their initial handshake – just like you and I did on the phone.

This first part of the protocol goes by the fancy name of transmission control protocol. But it is more commonly known as the TCP part of the well-known TCP/IP protocol suite.

To be compatible with industry speak, we'll simply refer to the overall process here as the Internet protocol, or just IP. And just as I explained to the attendees in my security seminar, every computer scientist must recognize IP as the foundational basis for practical computer communication, sort of like the periodic table in chemistry.

"The (Internet protocol) has become the de facto computer communications standard," writes Ed Skoudis in his book, *Counter Hack*, "the lingua franca of computers."

By the way, the Internet protocol works exactly the same in China and Italy, as it does in Indiana. When you type 'www dot some-computer-in-Iceland', your computer and the one in Iceland follow the exchange of numbers we just outlined. The owners of both machines must be using compatible software to do this. But this software comes with your Internet browser or email program. You don't have to do a thing.

Remember that the phone and Internet protocols are reliant on both parties following the rules agreed upon in advance. That is, just as it would cause problems if I called you on the phone and remained silent or did something unexpected after you answered, computers can also be configured to confuse the Internet protocol interaction. This can range from sending bogus random numbers to forging Internet protocol address information.

As we alluded to in earlier discussions, the most devastating protocol security violation involves a denial of service attack. In such an attack, one party sends a barrage of information to another computer. This is done so quickly that the receiving end has no time to keep up.

The distributed version of the denial of service attack (DDOS) involves the compromise of many vulnerable systems to accomplish the attack. One might view this as akin to asking a group of people to begin shouting at some victim all at once. The noise coming from the distributed sources becomes overwhelming, and this is precisely what happens in a DDOS attack.

But denial of service is not the only way to cause problems with the Internet protocol. Computers identify themselves by attaching their Internet address to the messages being sent, just as you would with a letter you pop in the mail. Special types of computers called routers that reside across the Internet, direct these messages to the recipient, also designated by address information on the message.

An attack called a spoof involves a sending party placing phony address information on messages. That is, if your real network address is XYZ, then you change it to something other than XYZ in the hopes of maybe tricking the recipient. Suppose, for instance, that the recipient has security controls which allow only computers from certain addresses to gain entry, then an attacker might use this knowledge to try to get in.

Such an attack is reminiscent of Abbie Hoffman's clever suggestion in 1970 that you mail a letter to your mother with her address as the sending address. Then, when you conveniently forget to put stamps on the letter (wink, wink), it is returned to your mother marked 'insufficient postage', and you will have gotten the letter to her without paying.

In both the Internet protocol attack and Abbie Hoffman's postal rip-off, the attacker lies about a source identity in order to trick the underlying protocol. This is a common problem and currently has no commonly agreed upon solution on the Internet.

Insider Sabotage

Security experts have long recognized the challenges that organizations face in keeping insiders from sabotaging systems using proprietary knowledge. We all know that in any business or government agency, you ultimately have to trust someone. So if terrorists manage to become trusted insiders in a company that controls or manages critical infrastructure, then the implications can be frightening.

"Experience and statistics have clearly shown," writes Kevin Mitnick in his book, *The Art of Deception*, "that the greatest threat to the enterprise is from insiders. It's the insiders who have intimate knowledge of where the valuable information resides, and where to hit the company to cause the most harm."

Here's a scenario for you to consider: Let's suppose that you're an evil cyber terrorist working for some company that produces air traffic control software. Your specific assignment, perhaps from your terrorist sponsor, was to join this company for the purpose of eventually injecting a trap door into the software.

Now, after years of patient preparation, it's finally time to complete the assignment. A team of experts, also connected to your sponsor, developed the trap door. They did a fine job – it's an elegant design, small and compact. Your job is to now slip the trap door into the code just after final testing.

Since you've risen during your quiet tenure to a highly trusted position, slipping in this trap door will be easy. Once it is in, your associates will be able to trigger failures in the software any time they wish. In essence, you've planted a time bomb, one that will remain hidden until it is activated. You will also go completely unnoticed as the source of this problem. You might even retire with a gold watch.

Keep in mind that malicious insiders could be motivated by deeply held personal or nationalistic beliefs. This will fuel their intensity and determination to successfully undermine an operation. Juergen Mohammed Gietler, an archivist for the German Foreign

Ministry, was caught in 1991 passing western military and political intelligence to Iraq. After serving his sentence, he explained on *CBS 60 Minutes* that he felt it was his national duty to leak this information.

Insider access is also an effective way to bypass the security perimeter model that so many organizations try to employ. Specifically, the perimeter model involves placing security devices such as firewalls around the edge of an organization's network systems, not unlike the posting of guards around some large physical complex.

Since most organizations tend to trust what goes on inside their perimeter, internal security protections are often quite lax. Thus, an insider might have unfettered access to all of the information and resources that exist inside the perimeter. In fact, I'd bet a paycheck that the first massive Digital Pearl Harbor-type cyber attack on national infrastructure (and let's hope this never happens) includes a healthy dose of insider access.

Here's a story: Several years ago, I was being given a tour of the software operations location for a large organization in the Far East. We eventually got to one of the big rooms where the programmers worked. In this room, everyone was seated next to one another in row after row, gazing into their computer monitors, and clicking away at their keyboards. The clatter made the place sound like an old New York newsroom.

At the front of the room sat a rather serious looking manager who reminded me of my grammar school principle. He had the same stern expression, with his glasses rested at the tip of his nose. I watched as he sat there flipping through a stack of computer paper – the wide variety that used to come out of line printers in 1980. This mountain of printout paper was probably six inches high.

"Is that the boss?" I asked my host.

"Oh, no," he replied, laughing. "That man is from security. Those are log files he's flipping through."

"Log files?"

"Yes. We monitor the activity of all our programmers. The information is fed into log files which we examine to uncover any type of fraudulent or inappropriate behavior."

I scratched my head. "Can he really pick anything up in those printouts?"

Again, my host laughed. "Probably not," he replied with a great smile. "But I don't think our employees will be taking any chances."

I wish I could tell you that most national infrastructure security teams do a better job of dealing with insider security than this scheme. But the truth is that most countries and businesses have no solution to insider sabotage. The typical process of background checks and polygraph examinations certainly helps, but it is insufficient against a determined effort to gain insider access.

In fact, the only truly effective means for dealing with insiders is to first assume that they are present in our businesses and government agencies. This has the effect of requiring that all security systems in an organization be designed to presume that malicious attackers are nearby. It changes the security game in a fundamental way.

Simple Cyber Attack Model

At this point, we should examine the typical steps involved in most malicious cyber attacks.[9]

Our generic attack description will be written from the perspective of the attacker. That is, we'll present the attack steps as if we've climbed into the mind of the attacker. Because most of these steps are accomplished quietly and gradually, cyber security defenders of infrastructure will see the effects of attacks quite differently.

---

[9] Obviously, no two cyber attacks are ever the same, so the best we can do is approximate the steps in a typical sort of attack.

Step 1: Reconnaissance

Cyber attacks – like bank robberies and jewelry heists – begin with the collection of information on some target. Crooks on television call this casing the joint. (By the way, Google Earth allows you to case a joint in Africa from a bedroom in Iowa.)

For an insider, collecting sensitive information on an enterprise network is trivial because no organizations, outside military and intelligence environments, ever compartmentalize their knowledge base. For outsiders, the collection process is also fairly straightforward. Information about a target infrastructure can be easily obtained through Web surfing, search engines, trips to the library, viewing of television and news reports, government documents and studies, and even some directed inquiries.

As an example, during the first Gulf War with Iraq, General Norman Schwarzkopf called Colin Powell, who was then the Chairman of the Joint Chiefs of Staff, to complain that *Newsweek's* description of his flank plans was much too accurate for his comfort. Powell's response was not to worry, because so many different articles existed describing so many different plans that the enemy would have trouble figuring out which one was correct. Makes you feel pretty safe, doesn't it?

I routinely shake my head at books and articles that provide too much detailed information about infrastructure. In one *Atlantic Monthly* article, the reader was treated to a detailed description of the physical entry methods into a specifically named facility in a specifically named company. This was particularly startling since the company highlighted in the article sold security services.

A government official once told me that citizens with Internet connections have access to more complete and accurate intelligence today than professional analysts had a dozen years ago. This information doesn't even have to be currently on-line. Google's cache, for example, stores a great deal of information that may have been removed from the Internet, but can still be searched through its persistent storage. Furthermore, the Freedom of Information Act (FOIA) in the United States, allows anyone to obtain juicy information from the Federal Government on virtually anything.

Let's not forget that cyber attackers will also resort to more marginal means for obtaining information. Here's an all-too-typical scenario: Let's say that you are a struggling system administrator working in a company that supports a critical infrastructure function, perhaps in telecommunications. You are worried about your job and, in fact, your company is announcing lay-offs.

So you do what any normal person would do: You start looking for another job. You notice that a nearby employment group is advertising positions for people with your background. You call them and set up an interview. During the interview, they grill you on the details of which technologies you use, and the types of projects you're involved with on a day-to-day basis at your company. They tell you that their clients are very demanding about detail and they need specifics.

You're surprised and impressed that they have enough technical knowledge to ask you such detailed questions. You can hardly believe that they can comment so intelligently as you go to the white board in their office and diagram the computer and network configuration you manage. They ask relevant questions and you are convinced that you have picked the right search firm.

You're especially pleased with yourself after the interview since you've been able to answer every question asked. You are told that you were the best candidate to have been interviewed in some time. You leave fully confident that the discussion has been a total success. But after the interview, weeks pass without any subsequent contact from them. You try to call, but it appears their phone has been disconnected. You presume that they've gone out of business.

But have they really? Or have they simply moved on to some other city where they will perform this reconnaissance scam on others in similar circumstances. You've given them information that is the equivalent of gold to criminals, competitors, and cyber terrorist attack cells. It's a fairly old trick. (By the way, for obvious reasons, this is also something you would be very unlikely to report to the corporate security department in your company.)

As you would guess, the result of this reconnaissance process is a complete dossier on some target, perhaps a company or a government agency. Cyber terrorists would build this dossier focused mostly on computer and network-based information; however, in a broadly sponsored activity, such a dossier would probably be woven in the context of a much larger reconnaissance activity.

Let's suppose that the reconnaissance target is a private business that supplies engineering and program management services to some critical infrastructure element in government. Defense contractors building weapons come to mind as a prime example. They are often filled with insiders who have recently left the military, but who are still quite current in their knowledge.

The dossier on this target government contracting firm might include information about the types of technologies and applications being used in the company, information about the employees (especially their phone numbers and email addresses), processes that are used within the company, distribution channels for products and services, and on and on.

Some years ago, at an aerospace conference open only to individuals with United States Government secret clearances, a contractor behind one of the booths noticed an individual wandering around the floor without a badge. This contractor approached the individual who responded with the dubious claim that he was covering the event for a foreign newspaper. Subsequent investigation showed this to be utter nonsense, and that this person regularly scouted foreign technology for his country.

The bottom line is that information reconnaissance will almost certainly occur at the beginning of the cyber attack cycle, but in a manner largely invisible to cyber security methods. Sure, we can all exercise more diligence in keeping sensitive information more private. But unless someone is willing to shut down all the search engines, cyber security attacks will have to be countered in some later attack phase.[10]

Step 2: Scanning

The second step in a cyber attack involves the use of tools to perform active scanning on target infrastructure.

Where reconnaissance involves the broad collection of background information from many different sources, scanning involves much more focused and directed queries aimed at specific computers and networks to see what sort of vulnerabilities might be present. Sometimes people refer to scanning as doorknob rattling, but it's done much more remotely and anonymously over a network.

Here's how it works. A malicious individual or group starts the process by obtaining scanning software. Such software can be purchased from a security product vendor, or downloaded for free on the Internet. Most information security departments in companies and government agencies buy scanning tools to use on themselves for security purposes. A scanner is thus designed to systematically connect over a network to any computer services that are available.

Explosions in the use of wireless technology have led to the development of air-based scanners. Sometimes these scanners are run on a corporate network with the intention of finding access points to wireless networks. I've even seen security guards wander around buildings in the evening with handheld scanners looking for open networks. Other times a laptop is used to simply connect to whatever can be found in the vicinity. The result can be somewhat alarming.

Listen to this typical description of wireless scanning activity from a hacker: "We used a Cisco card, magmount antenna on the roof, a Garmin GPS, and Kismet," writes Dragorn in a *2600*

---

[10] By the way, the notion of rigging search engines to detect and trace suspicious queries is ridiculous. Aside from the obvious ethical, social, and legal problems, it would provide utter nonsense in the way of intelligence.

Magazine, article. "In an hour and a half, we found 448 networks. In the center of Manhattan, an area which arguably should be more security aware than anywhere else, only 26 percent of the networks had encryption enabled. At least 75 of the access points were factory configurations, with all the default access granted."

(One can't help but imagine the late, great Richard Feynmann smirking down from Heaven at this ridiculously insecure situation. I'll bet he'd joke that the security managers of such insecure networks would protect their networks by keeping everyone out of Manhattan.)

The process of scanning a network – wireless or otherwise – is quite simple. In fact, it's basically what you do when you browse the Internet. Your browser finds a computer located at some designated address and checks to see if Web services are available. If so, then you see Web content; if not, then you get an error message.

Scanners follow the same process. They search through designated addresses looking for connected devices, and then determine what services are available on these devices. Like a search engine, they might go out and search for specific content. In fact, imagine your search engine trying to find security vulnerabilities, and you have a very rough idea of how a scanner operates.

Here's the kicker: If you set up a remote access service to your computer, or if you connect directly to the Internet, scanners will find you. In fact, the typical machine connected to the public Internet will see automated scanning activity within minutes of being connected. This is particularly true if you have an always-on broadband connection to your computer. Scanning activity will have a better shot at finding and hitting your system if it is bound to an address for a longer period of time.

A few years ago, my security team was hired by a major corporation to run security scans on their entire enterprise. We did this with computer and phone scanners that looked for anything connected to a dial up modem. Over a weekend, we were able to make so much headway into their enterprise, that we could actually get into their operations systems and make changes to critical systems.

What was happening was that their employees were violating company security policy and connecting their computers to modems in their offices. This allowed them to conveniently access their files from home; but it also provided a wide open door for attack – and this company happened to be in the air travel industry. You might pause for a moment to consider the cyber terrorist possibilities of this sort of thing in a post-9/11 traveling environment.

When people administer their computers poorly, they make the cyber terrorist's scanning activity easier. For example, terrorists often use scanners to find computers that can be used as dupes. That is, they'll search the Internet for poorly administered computers with broadband connections. Some software vulnerability is then exploited and malicious code is placed onto each machine. During all of this, the computer owners have no clue that anything is happening. After all, what percentage of computer owners are professional system administrators?

Anyway, once this has been done to many thousands of dupe machines, the terrorist issues a command and the dupes begin an attack on the target victim. Generally, the process is controlled by a compromised Internet connected server, often referred to as a bot controller. The process is difficult for law enforcement, because the attacks seem to emanate from thousands of different "average Joe" computers with broadband connections.

More recently, these attacks have been connected to extortion demands. That is, attackers will aim a denial of service attack at a victim, and will offer to make it stop if some ransom is paid. The amount is generally not huge – it might be anything from a five to ten thousand dollars. Once the money is transferred to an anonymous account, the attack then stops. Many groups elect to pay the fine. Others do not. It remains unclear which is the right decision in the long term.

The best alternative to avoid paying the ransom is to employ one's service provider to filter the attack. Service providers have a unique vantage point in all of this, because attacks traverse their infrastructure. As such, they can often use special security techniques to stop denial of service attacks. Unfortunately, however, this practice is not widespread among carriers.[11]

As you might guess, like reconnaissance, scanning is a difficult attack step to completely deflect or stop. But under the right circumstances, it can be detected. Many of the security measures we'll describe in later chapters will be focused on the detection and response to specific types of scanning that proceed on the Internet.

Step 3: Access

The third step in the cyber attack process involves actually gaining access to systems by exploiting vulnerabilities gathered during reconnaissance and scanning.

As a young Bell Labs security engineer, I remember being called with my associates into Unix pioneer Bob Morris Sr.'s office. He announced boldly that promptly at such-and-such time on that afternoon, he would break into the Bell Labs Computer Center in Whippany. I couldn't wait to see what he would do. It was hard to concentrate that day.

Anyway, we all finally crowded behind him at the designated time, and we watched carefully as he cracked his knuckles, leaned over his keyboard, and went tappety-tappety-tap, tappety-tappety-tap into his dumb terminal (you didn't point and click much in those days). Then, he leaned back and let us look over his shoulder at the written gibberish on the screen.

"See," he boasted with a broad grin. "I'm in."

---

[11] Service providers refer to this as blackholing. It involves redirecting bad packet streams away from a target. More recent tools have emerged that filter only the bad portion of the stream, so that the good portion can progress.

I craned my neck to look at what the Unix system was displaying on his terminal. Most of it looked like a bunch of Chinese to me at the time.

"Hacking operating systems is simple," he boasted further, leaning back in his chair. "Trivial, in fact."

I looked more carefully. Sure enough, I could see that he did have a root shell, which gave him full access to the Unix operating system. He could delete files, add new users, change system passwords, shut down services, or pretty much anything else you could think of.

At the time, none of us had a clue how he did this, but it was certainly inspiring. It also helped us understand the role of vulnerabilities in system attack. Once you are aware of the vulnerabilities, also known as soft spots, in a target system, then you can often gain totally unimpeded access to virtually anything.

By the way, in case you're wondering, I believe that the vulnerability that Morris was exploiting involved redefining the internal field separators (IFS) like spaces and tabs used to separate words in a command to the computer. I won't get into the details here, but it allowed him to trick the computer into executing a system command that would provide access. This attack doesn't work now, but it sure worked great in its day.

The soft spots where cyber terrorists will focus include obvious things like remote login accounts and passwords. Soft spots are also created when obvious security protections are simply not in place. As an example, a soft spot is created by a wide-open Internet connection without a firewall. Companies that do not attend to security make it easy for terrorists to find soft spots.

The great Doug McIlroy, one of the original masters of the Unix operating system at Bell Labs, told the story once about a demonstration he'd given during the early Seventies at a university in Canada. Dialing over the public telephone network to his computer in New Jersey, he performed the demonstration live. Several weeks later, however, he noticed odd behavior on his system. A bit of investigation uncovered that students from the university had looked at their phone bill to determine the number McIlroy had dialed. They used this to gain access to his unprotected system.

Soft spots can also include time bomb code placed in software applications. Terrorist insiders might introduce these as part of their jobs administering your software. They might also introduce bombs while developing the software, an approach that has huge consequences for mass market software. Time bomb code works by triggering on some condition or period of elapsed time, after which some predetermined action occurs. It might be designed to delete information, corrupt files, or whatever.

Such sabotage is especially frightening when you consider that most organizations sent their software out to special companies and consultants for pre-Y2K remediation in 1999. I wonder how many of these organizations checked to make sure that no time bomb code was placed inside their code. The answer is most likely zero.

To summarize, this third step in our attack model is directed at a given target and requires an explicit set of actions aimed at that target. As such, it is somewhat detectable, and most computer security methods focus specifically on this step. Access controls, passwords, network security methods, and the like are all designed to make sure that proper access policies are enforced. Needless to say, with buggy software and poor system administration so common, these controls are rarely perfect.

Step 4: Damage

The fourth step in a cyber attack involves using the unauthorized access gained in the previous step to cause real damage. Such damage would come in the form of either disclosure, integrity, denial of service, or theft activity.

Security experts agree that when access is obtained on a target system, very little often remains in the form of useful security prevention. It is certainly possible to set up a security system that detects slight changes in authorized use in a given system (perhaps signaling an intrusion). Such systems, called host-based intrusion detection systems, are designed to collect information about a typical computing or networking environment. This information is then used as a baseline to determine what is normal versus what is not.

The concept is reasonably sound in environments that are predictable. But it is much more difficult to make this approach work in environments where establishing a normal baseline is impossible. Furthermore, host based intrusion detection might be subverted when a bad person has administrative access to a system. That person can go in and clean up any evidence of tampering that might exist in log files.

In considering the type of damages than can affect an organization, system managers must determine which assets are critical. That is, if the manager of some system had to select a base set of assets that could be protected by some catastrophic event, which ones would they be? Sometimes with my graduate students, I'll pose the following scenario to help them understand the essence of identifying one's critical assets:

Imagine that you have one minute to enter your home to grab your most important belongings. Once you've come out with your selections, we push a bomb detonator (don't worry, this is just a thought experiment). The bomb, however, has only a fifty-fifty chance of actually going off. If it goes off, then oh well. But if it doesn't, then you play another round. We repeat this until you've either cleaned out your apartment or the place blows up.

When I ask my students what they'd grab in the first round, most select things like pets, cash, heirlooms, and jewelry. The key here is that they select assets that are not easily replaced. In subsequent rounds, additional considerations like convenience and preference can be introduced. But in this first round, one is advised to grab things that are not replaceable. (Surprisingly, most students grab their iPods in the first round. Perhaps this says something about their price.)

The point of this whimsical scenario should be obvious: In order to properly assess the potential damage that a cyber attack might cause to infrastructure, one must first recognize what is important in that infrastructure. If an attack does not target the most critical assets, then its effects will be much less severe.

From the perspective of national infrastructure protection, such identification of critical assets is a controversial topic. In the United States, for instance, the government has encouraged industry sectors to share information with each other – and with government – so that accurate determinations can be made of national risk to critical assets.

This is a reasonable goal, but organizations often worry about sharing sensitive information. If detailed understanding were obtained by terrorists of the vital assets that existed in critical cyber infrastructure systems – including locations of back up systems, key vulnerabilities, protection weaknesses, and so on – then the negative effects could be severe during a cyber attack. Such disclosure happens more often than it should, and the effects can only be bad.

Step 5: Hide Tracks

The fifth step in a cyber attack involves covering up any incriminating evidence that may have been left behind. This could be on the attack target or any intermediary system.

Intruders have known for years that when they perform reconnaissance, scanning, access, or tampering, evidence is always left behind somewhere. This can occurs directly through the use of logs that keep track of behavior on a given system. The log output is known as an audit trail, and intruders understand that when they attack a system, they must hide their tracks if they wish to avoid being caught.

During the investigation of the infamous Oklahoma City bomber, it turned out that some unexpected information was made available to law enforcement. A video image from a local ATM camera picked up a Ryder truck passing by the Regency Towers in Oklahoma City just minutes before the Murrah Building was bombed. This image helped investigators piece together exactly what had happened.

Keep in mind that the image only helped with *post-attack* forensics. It did nothing preventive. Furthermore, no one would ever seriously expect ATM cameras to be used to prevent crimes that might be occurring in the vicinity. This seemingly obvious point is profound, and must be understood about cyber terrorism: Passive surveillance and log file collection and processing methods provide evidence, but do little to stop an attack from occurring.[12]

But perhaps this is not completely true. Sometimes the known existence of surveillance has a preventive effect on behavior. Here's a simple scenario: Suppose a late night bout of insomnia has you doing what most students of computer security do under such circumstances: You get up and stare into a glowing computer monitor, having a peek around the campus network.

In the course of your poking, you happen to find the computer server that your professor connects onto and uses every day. And, by chance, you happen to notice a directory on this machine labeled with your professor's name.

Interesting, you think to yourself. *I wonder what files are stored in this directory.*

So, you tappety-tap here and clickety-click there, and before you can say the phrase 'breaking and entering,' you're gazing at a list of files that belong to your professor. You also notice that one of the files is named 'midterm,' and it just so happens that you're having a midterm exam tomorrow. You look at the file details and realize that it was created today.

If you simply do not care about getting caught, then the issue of whether an audit trail can be used to uncover your activity is moot.

---

[12] Early detection of indicators can help prevent attack if the security infrastructure is mature and well designed. This is harder than you might imagine.

This is an important point, because we know that many cyber terrorists will not care a bit about whether their activity is detected.

In the case of the school examination, however, we must presume that you would want to avoid being caught. Hence, if you knew that log files were being created with a list of your activity, you would probably not go any further. We would say that, in this case, the logging system has a preventive effect.

Future cyber terrorist attacks will probably involve groups taking full credit for their malicious actions. As a result, the issue of covering tracks as a phase in a cyber terrorist attack may be less critical to include in our overall critical infrastructure protection strategy. We must instead take steps to prevent attackers from even having the opportunity to cover their tracks.

3 Effects Of Cyber Attacks

COMPUTER SECURITY EXPERTS HAVE A FAVORITE, albeit somewhat worn, joke question that they never seem to tire of posing to unsuspecting victims. Here's how it goes:

"So, have you ever been hacked?" asks the cyber security expert to the unknowing victim.

"Uh, no. We haven't been hacked," goes the response.

The expert then raises an eyebrow.

"You mean, there haven't been any attacks that you've *noticed*."

The point here, in case you missed it, is that you cannot measure what you do not observe. So, anytime someone says that they've never been hacked, you can challenge their claim as outlined above (hopefully without having to repeat this bad joke).

With this consideration in mind, I will state that to my knowledge no one has ever *noticed* catastrophic problems for government or business infrastructure as a result of cyber attack. Perhaps a massive e-catastrophe is occurring right now under our noses, but its effects have not yet been noticed. Again, you cannot measure or even comment on what you do not notice; my point is that nothing of enormous consequence and reach has been noticed.

Certainly, we have seen our share of cyber security-related effects across a range of computer and network systems. Peter Neumann from SRI International moderates a comprehensive list of reported risks to the public from computer malfunction and attack. A brief perusal of his list (Internet search terms: Neumann, Risks) shows immediately that the effects of cyber security can be considerable.

Some familiar examples: Companies regularly get hacked and their email services are corrupted, especially by phishing attacks. Government agencies experience breaches that disrupt the services they offer. A school grading system is compromised by a thirteen-year-old who gives himself an 'A' in Earth Science. Individuals have their PCs infected with viruses that make it hard to run applications normally. Networks get infected with worms that cause volumes of packets to bring processing to a screeching halt. The list goes on and on.

In spite of these examples, we must acknowledge that while businesses, governments, and individuals have felt the negative impact of cyber attack, no digital Pearl Harbor cyber attack has been broadly noticed in any country or business. At the risk of beating a dead horse, we repeat that this *does not* mean that such attacks cannot ever occur. It just means that one probably hasn't happened yet – thankfully.

Four Types of Security Threats

If you were enrolled in my graduate course on cyber security at the Stevens Institute of Technology, you'd learn during the first lecture that the effects of cyber security attacks come in four flavors: disclosure, theft, integrity, and denial of service. Here is a brief list of what each entails:

Disclosure: This is when secret information leaks to the bad guys. This information could be credit card numbers, government secrets, battle plans, or your latest video rentals. The disclosure threat can cause a range of impacts from personal embarrassment to national security consequences.

Theft: This involves something of value being stolen. Network service providers worry quite a bit about this problem, which they refer to as fraud. In the telecommunications industry, fraud protection has matured steadily over the past few years – primarily to avoid lost revenue.

Integrity: This threat involves an asset being intentionally damaged. Examples include your PC being corrupted, files being infected, or some system attribute being changed. Any time a virus gets into your computer and causes problems, that is an integrity threat.

Denial of Service: This is when some service is intentionally blocked. This usually involves the denial of authorized access to network service or telephony. Some experts believe this to be the most difficult of all threats to deal with effectively.

As we will see, security in computing is thus not some monolithic notion, but rather a spectrum of damage that can occur with respect to computer and network systems. "Bad things," writes Ian Witten in a classic 1987 essay about cyber security, "range from minor but rankling irritations, through theft of information, to holding users ransom."

For example, consider that the theft of someone's personal identity is quite different from the theft of wartime logistic information – even though both would be referred to as security issues. Similarly, blocked access to a financial Web site is quite different from blocked access to a children's game site. In either case, a very different constituency (and age group) would be targeted in the attack. Furthermore, different attack motivations and methods would be employed in the security solution.

To properly understand the true consequences of cyber attack, we need to zero in on these four different types of security threat – focusing on their history, impacts, likelihood, and preventive measures. The resultant insight will not only help the reader better understand cyber security, but will also highlight some serious public issues for the protection of critical infrastructure.

Disclosed Secrets

The disclosure threat involves sensitive information falling into the hands of bad guys. In the context of national cyber attack, bad guys are probably a given nation's hated enemies. For Americans, this could range from al Qaeda terrorists, to organized cyber attack groups stealing information from sensitive government or corporate systems.

Ordinary individuals tend to worry about disclosure in the context of their personal information. Imagine, for a moment, that you've left a copy of your tax return papers on the copy machine at the office. You'd probably drive fifty miles in the dead of night to retrieve it. The obvious problem is that when this sort of information is available on-line, then all the driving in the dead of night will provide no protection whatsoever. Furthermore, an on-line attack doesn't require proximity.

One curious and rarely discussed aspect of people's private lives involves on-line browsing habits. If a person's browsing habits are mundane, then compromise might be of no consequence. But for those who enjoy visiting more marginal sites, this information is often best kept private. Your service provider, for example, should protect this information from prying eyes – including those of their own employees. "There's a fine line between customer service and stalking," writes cryptography expert Bruce Schneier.

In the mid 1970's, United States government researchers began seriously studying the disclosure threat as it related to computers. This early research wasn't so much concerned with personal information as it was with traditional Cold War tensions. As a result, the vast majority of early disclosure research was preoccupied with the threat that the Russians would use computers to peek at American military secrets.

Two creative researchers from the Mitre Corporation, David Bell and Len LaPadula, were among the first to publish meaningful results in this area. They examined how the United States military protected paper documents. They looked at the process of document classification, which allowed the military to define which people could gain access to which types of information. They found that a document classified as top-secret, for example, could only be read by someone with a top-secret clearance. Similarly, an unclassified document could be read by anyone.

Bell and LaPadula quickly realized that this disclosure concept could be applied to the multi-user, shared computers that were coming into use at the time. Their approach worked roughly as follows: All of the information on a shared computer would be marked to some security classification, such as secret or top-secret. Then, all users on that system would be associated with clearances, generally based on their background or job function. The operating system on the computer would enforce the desired security policy.

In practice, things were more slightly complicated because the military partitions information into "need-to-know" categories. Thus, within the top-secret classification, data must be compartmentalized into more specialized groupings. To manage the complexity, most classified government projects – then and now – employ teams of people to keep the security scheme straight. Bell and LaPadula knew that the computer version of this would require similar administration.

Some Unix-based computer operating systems were actually built in the 1980's to implement this type of military security policy. At AT&T, Chuck Flink led an effort aimed at trying to get the concept correct for Unix. The resulting system, referred to as multilevel secure, could enforce the familiar policy that highly cleared users could read any file in any directory, but that lowly cleared users were restricted to less sensitive information. Thus, a user would have to be cleared to top-secret to open and read a top-secret document. So far, so good.

But the policy also stipulated that highly cleared users could not write information into lesser-classified documents. This ensured that classified information didn't find its way into an unclassified document. An assumption was being made here that users logged into the system in "top-secret" mode, could only generate top-secret information. This is not a reasonable assumption, but it was made nevertheless.

Furthermore, the policy allowed for lesser-cleared individuals to write content to pretty much anything they wanted. After all, what was the harm in unclassified information making its way into a classified document? The result of this was the weird anomaly that unclassified users could write information into a top-secret document, but could not then read or review what they had written. This was called a blind write. (Are you confused yet?)

The clumsiness and inconvenience of such operation, combined with a generally low concern for computer security across the globe at the time, dealt multilevel secure systems a painful blow. As the public Internet and the Web emerged, most computer users' tolerance for restriction of information grew even lower. After all, what was the Internet for, other than to share, rather than restrict access to data? Products that supported military disclosure functionality died slow and painful deaths.

Since that early research, very little progress has been made in the prevention of disclosure threats on computers. Some researchers have since created more refined mathematical models of disclosure based on how people deduce information. But to be honest, very few people in the computing community even noticed this work. It didn't help that most of these papers could only be understood by people with PhD degrees in very specialized branches of mathematics.

Encryption has certainly been one method that has been used at length to try to prevent disclosure problems. Encrypting data has always worked especially well for information that is in transit. The military encrypts voice, for instance, using special "secure" phones. To listen in, the enemy would have to tap and decrypt the information in real-time – a task that has proven particularly difficult for good encryption methods.

When information is stored, however, encryption protection hasn't proven as dependable. One reason is that the keys used to decrypt stored information must be stored. If these keys are lost or mishandled, the information could be lost forever. This leads to baroque escrow schemes in which third parties keep emergency copies of the key information. Law enforcement has taken the extra step of suggesting that such escrowed keys could be used to decipher encrypted conversations. As you might guess, this has not been a popular suggestion.

In spite of all this, organizations have not stopped trying to create encryption schemes for protecting both their in-transit and stored information. The payment card industry, for example, recently enacted a series of privacy-oriented security requirements on its participants. These requirements include provision for encrypting all customer sensitive data. This turns out to be especially difficult for legacy applications that include no support for such encryption.

Ironically, many of the companies in this industry have wasted more time complaining about the problems implementing encryption than they have actually trying to create a workable scheme. Time will tell whether encryption of stored information has much impact on prevention of privacy problems.[13]

The potential disclosure of information in enterprise networks run by organizations is often addressed poorly as well. Most companies tend to operate their entire network at one common security level – usually something related to proprietary markings. In most companies, the perimeter of the organizational Intranet is the vehicle for such protection. So, if you are a legitimate employee, then you can see everything; otherwise you aren't able to see anything – or at least that's the intent.

The perimeter protection of an Intranet is typically accomplished using devices called firewalls. The sad news is that firewalls can be penetrated or by-passed quite easily in most environments. Furthermore, Intranets are notorious for having unauthorized and unknown connections to the outside through which bad guys can

---

[13] By the way, disclosure issues, in a personal context, are referred to collectively as privacy.

gain access and peek at information (Hint: think WiFi). As a result, disclosure protections in many organizations are little more than a sham.

Suppose, for example, that you are an evil criminal and you want to obtain intellectual property and sensitive information from Bank XYZ. You could try to hack your way in, but that might be messy. Perhaps a better approach would be to just apply for a job at the bank. Then, once you're at your new job, you build a volume of downloaded information from their Intranet (you're an employee, remember?). After you have what you want, you can quit and move on to the next bank. It's reasonably foolproof in most environments.

For information stored on PCs, the disclosure threat is addressed through mostly non-technical means. Specifically, most people will try to delete what they do not think they need, such as their temporary Internet files and any cookies that might reside on their hard drive. They will then protect the remaining files and data by simply turning off the PC and, if it's a laptop, storing it in the closet.

We all know, however, that when PCs are connected to networks, they are immediately exposed to all sorts of security threats. This is not to say that every time you connect your PC to the Internet hackers peek in at your checking account, but there are often no controls to ensure that this cannot happen.

Theft

Suppose that a well-dressed young man hops aboard a southbound Amtrak train in Baltimore. It's very early in the morning, and hardly anyone else is on the train. The conductor comes over to the passenger requesting a ticket, but the young man pleads for mercy.

"Sir, I don't have a ticket because I don't have any money," he explains. "I'm on my way to an interview in Washington. This is my big chance. Can you please let me ride without paying?"

The conductor frowns.

"Please, sir," the young man pleads. "There aren't many other passengers in this entire car. I'm not bothering anyone. My presence is having absolutely no negative effect on the operation of this train. Can't you please let me ride down to my interview in Washington for free?"

The conductor takes off his cap and scratches his head as he ponders this little dilemma. What harm, he wonders, is this kid really causing? He knows that Amtrak is a big company and if the young man is allowed to ride for free, maybe some good will come if it. Maybe he will even bring the money back later, after he gets his job.[14]

This train conductor's dilemma is similar to the fraud decisions that security engineers must make as they ponder the impacts of theft. Service providers, in particular, have been forced to consider such scenarios in great detail. The services in question are most often telephony or Internet access, and the excuses for theft are just as creative and real as we saw with the young man riding the train to Washington.

You probably already know that theft of phone and Internet services is so common that some youngsters believe it to be a socially acceptable activity. The early activist Abbie Hoffman urged his followers to rip off the phone company at every opportunity. Today, the hacking community openly targets telecommunications in their mischievous explorations. In response, most phone companies today have established large security and fraud divisions that deal on a day-to-day basis with people trying to steal service.

It turns out that stopping fraud on the Internet is a bit more difficult than with traditional voice services. The identity and location of end points, for example, are tough to accurately determine on the Internet. Furthermore, the motivation to stop Internet theft is somewhat more complex than with voice service. For example, if someone is stealing expensive minutes on your long distance service, then it pays to stop this. But if someone is stealing time on an

---

[14] When I pose this scenario to my students, the responses are split between throwing the bum off and showing mercy. I have no idea what this means other than that half are destined for upper management (I won't say which half).

Internet or voice account that is already flat rate for unlimited use, then what's the problem? Would you even notice if someone was occasionally borrowing your on-line account to browse the Web?

Identity theft is the newest form of cyber theft, and it is rather alarming in its potential consequences. The most common identity theft method involves the use of a technique known as *phishing*. In a typical phishing scam, email notifications are sent to unsuspecting users that they must take some immediate action, such as re-enrolling for their Internet service by supplying personal information. Bogus Web sites on hacked systems are often established to support such theft operations.

"Warning," such messages might start, "to ensure the fine quality of service you are used to, you must immediately go to the following Web site (the link would be embedded) to verify your account information. We'll need your email password, your mother's maiden name, and your social security number. Failure to take this action immediately will result in your account being terminated."

Once the unsuspecting user visits the Web site and provides this private information, the thieves grab it, catalogue it, and sell it. Such information might end up in the hands of people who will charge items to your credit cards; or it could end up in the hands of criminals who sell identities on underground Web sites; or it could be placed in the hands of a cyber criminal using this information to establish anonymous on-line accounts. All of these are frightening prospects.

Unfortunately, few good solutions exist to stop phishing. A recent study in the State of New York showed a that sizeable percentage of employees sent a test phish, went ahead and took the bait. Many took the bait again, after being warned that the original phish was a test! So while end-user education and awareness campaigns are necessary, they don't always work too well.

One promising technique that has been discussed involves using stronger forms of authentication for any type of interaction between, say, a bank and its customers. The idea is that you would be issued something like a hardware token by the bank when you agree to do on-line banking. Thus, even if your identity were stolen via a phishing attack, the thieves would not be able to clean out your checking account unless they also had your hardware security token. This may be a good approach, but it has sizeable cost implications.

With the recent rush of phishing attacks, companies have now begun to take serious notice of the threat. While many companies remain ambivalent about employees being caught in identity theft scams, as phishing scams have expanded in scope, organizations now realize that viruses can be delivered to the enterprise via this technique.

The paradoxical result is that companies are now being forced to address fraud, not so much to protect the personal information of their employees, but rather to preserve the integrity of their corporate computer and network systems. Regardless of the motivation, one should expect the risk of identity theft and phishing problems to diminish for those who access the Internet from an organizational Intranet.

For normal citizens, one already sees service providers beginning to accept the task of protecting their users from these types of scams. Certainly, extensions to anti-virus and anti-Spam software packages exist to help identify theft situations in various types of malware, but the truth is that people remain pretty gullible. The only protection many Internet users will ever have is if some omnipotent provider steps in and makes the problem go away. This is not easy, but the benefit is significant enough that we should expect broadband providers to begin working this more aggressively.

In the meantime, my advice is that if you receive an email asking you to supply any sort of personal information, even if it appears to be coming from someone you trust, please reach for the delete key and just say no.

Destroying and Deleting Assets

Several years ago, a team of young New York paralegals had just finished working days and nights preparing a lengthy legal document. They'd worked like dogs getting every sentence perfect and every punctuation mark just so. After all, even a minor error in this document could change its meaning and cost the firm millions.

Just before the document was to be printed and delivered to the court, the paralegals were all called into a room and fired. While they were packing to leave, however, one person decided to take some revenge. He went back to the computer and made a few creative adjustments in the document – ones that would be tough to find. In computer security terms, we would say that the integrity of the overall document was degraded. Its validity was now in question and its contents could no longer be trusted.

This law firm might have protected themselves from such an attack by a few simple steps. Treating their employees with respect would have been a good start, since removing the motivation for an attack is always the best approach. But functional strategies do exist for ensuring integrity in a business-computing environment. They could have had back-ups; they could have had a change-tracking system; they could have been monitoring audit trails; they could have had access controls on the document to prevent unauthorized change; they could have had business controls on dealing with fired employees; the list goes on and on.

But the truth is that most companies and groups do not have decent protections from this integrity threat. Most organizations rarely back up anything but the most critical information. How often does the typical computer user, for instance, back up the routine files on their PC? Once a day? Once a week? Ever? Furthermore, unlike the disclosure threat, which received considerable attention in the early years of computer security, the integrity threat has been largely ignored by researchers and funding authorities.

Back in the 1970's, a Mitre researcher named Ken Biba was studying the integrity problem, largely from the perspective of protecting military systems. He came to the conclusion that integrity, unlike disclosure, was really just a measure of one's expectation. A person of high integrity, for example, is someone you can trust, someone who lives up to a high expectation. Similarly, a high integrity document is one that is correct, has value, and has not been tampered with.

Biba also observed that people with high integrity routinely avoided documents of low integrity. This is why we prevent children from viewing low integrity materials, like certain magazines and Web sites. If we did not take this preventive measure, then our children would be presumably corrupted and their integrity would be irrevocably reduced. Some people joke that exposure to low integrity materials causes us all to start life with the highest level of integrity – and then throughout our life, we embark on a constant process of ever-dropping integrity.

Low integrity individuals are also routinely prevented from contributing to high integrity documents. It's sort of like stopping a profane, vulgar person from changing passages in an important religious document. The information entered by the low integrity individual would have the effect of lowering the integrity of the document. A much better approach, of course, is to prevent this from occurring in the first place.

Biba tried to apply these observations to computer systems and interesting results emerged. One interesting Unix system developed at Bell Labs in the 1980's used Biba's approach to protect itself miraculously from worms.[15] It kept low integrity programs connected to networks from ever writing anything into the high integrity systems files. Bell-La Padula controls were then imposed upside-down to enforce the separation. The system gave you a bit of vertigo, but it worked like a charm.

---

[15] No one was writing worms at the time, so this technology was a solution with no associated problem.

You'd think that such functionality would be useful today. Unfortunately, systems like this didn't sell, because information technology managers deemed them too inconvenient. I wonder if these managers have since bothered to measure the inconvenience of responding to an endless stream of network viruses on their systems. Perhaps the inconvenience of using a more secure system might not seem so bad in comparison.

In the 1980's, another research project had some influence on our collective thinking about integrity in the cyber security community. The project was led by David Clark, a computer scientist from MIT, and David Wilson, from the accounting firm of Ernst and Whinney. Their work resulted in what we now know as the Clark Wilson Model. Several working groups were created in the late 1980's and early 1990's to determine how this model could be used to improve integrity protection on computer systems.

The model is based on the observation that the integrity of computing environments could benefit most from the types of things that businesses do to make sure their financial books remain in order. They explained that performing tasks such as ensuring valid transactions, logging all activity, ensuring good back-ups, and allowing only certain people to access certain important assets, would prove useful to engineers trying to ensure integrity.

The basis for the model is similar to how your checking account works. Every transaction you log in your checking account starts with all entries in a valid state (you hope). Once you complete a transaction, such as writing a check or making a deposit, you perform the associated log entry to make sure everything remains in a valid state.

Clark and Wilson reasoned that computer systems could be designed in the same way. Only valid transactions could be allowed to occur on systems that were already in a valid state. Mathematicians cleared things up for the masses by explaining that this part of the model produced something called "inductive closure."

Unfortunately, this concept turned out to be much easier said than done. How, for example, would you demonstrate validity for a PC running the Windows operating system and the usual set of popular applications? Or how could one ever state, for instance, that such a system is in a valid state if it must be patched every month? Or how could one ensure that only valid transactions are allowed to occur when viruses and other malware find their way onto our systems so easily?

In the end, the Clark-Wilson model was excellent theory, but too difficult to implement in practice. Most security experts are ignorant of the model, and almost no real systems have been built using the basic tenets of the model. This is a shame.

So how do we maintain integrity in computer systems? For the most part, we don't. People buy a home computer at Best Buy, plug it into the Internet and then use it to browse and send email. Over time, the system becomes increasingly muddled with viruses and Trojan horses. The anti-virus license expires, and soon the whole system becomes unusable. The result is that person goes out and buys a new system – and the cycle begins again. As you would guess, the computer industry has no problem with this approach.

Mind you, security tools do exist for detecting changes to a system. These tools often scan the target system periodically looking for anything that might have changed. A couple of decades ago, Fred Grampp from Bell Labs invented the first such program – one that scanned a Unix system for vulnerabilities. It checked for unused accounts, programs with too much system privilege, bad passwords, and so on. Computer system administrators do this routinely now, but the whole process traces it lineage to this early work at Bell Labs.

Now that I've said such nice things about Fred's scanning program, let me offer a sobering reality: a professional cyber terrorist can attack systems without breaking a sweat at scanners. Computer scanners are designed to test for known problems. If some previously unknown or unreported problem happens on your system, then a scanner will not be able to detect this in any way.[16]

You may not know this, but the software you buy for your home computer might be embedded with intentional Trojan horses before you even unwrap and install the software. These gems, referred to as Easter eggs by software developers, are inserted quietly into code and represent an artistic means for the authors to sign their work. For example, recent versions of Microsoft's Excel program could be turned into a flight program where you fly over bumpy terrain in search of an engraved stone. Engraved on this stone were the names of the developers.

Similarly, an earlier version of Microsoft's Word program could be turned into a pinball machine by a simple sequence of points, clicks, and simple text entry. I've demonstrated this frequently, and people are consistently floored at how little they understand about the software on their computers. Here is something I think we all agree on:

No justification exists for intentional Easter Eggs or Trojan horses, however innocent, to be placed in software by developers.

Unfortunately, no evidence exists that the integrity of critical infrastructure systems is protected more effectively than in home settings. This could be obvious, such as when a power plant or emergency service environment includes the types of virus-prone PCs you might find in the home. But it could also be more subtle, such as when custom developed software contains integrity problems due to insufficient levels of assurance and verification performed during development.

This does not mean that the most recent virus to hit your PC could also take out the computers in your local nuclear power plant. But you never know.

---

[16] Fred Grampp receives little credit for his pioneering work in scanning. Industries are based on concepts he invented – and people don't know his name.

Denying Service

The concept of denying service is easy for most people to grasp. See if any of the following analogous scenarios are familiar to you:

- You're in a rush to get to work, but the traffic is so thick you can barely move ten feet.

- You're trying to get onto an important conference call, but the signal on your cell phone is too weak to connect.

- You're watching the World Series and it's the ninth inning of a tie game during a crucial at-bat, and your satellite coverage suddenly goes out.

When these scenarios occur, we generally just resign ourselves to the fact that stuff happens. And we deal with it.

But imagine if in addition to your inconvenience, you also knew that someone was *deliberately* causing this situation. Imagine if that traffic jam was being caused intentionally to make you late. Of if your cell signal was being degraded for the sole purpose of keeping you off your call. Or if television coverage was shut down to keep you from watching your game. Such infuriating situations correspond to the denial of service threat.

Stated explicitly, denial of service in cyber security involves a malicious intruder intentionally blocking an important computer or network service from its authorized users. Note that denial of service does not correspond to accidental or unintentional outages. Rather, the threat involves someone causing the problem deliberately.

Examples of this abound. Perhaps you are a war fighter and need some on-line tactical information, only to find that the enemy is actively blocking your access. Or perhaps you run an emergency service, and during a serious life-threatening situation, you are blocked from accessing some important system by some hacker. Or maybe your shipping business allows customers to check package delivery on-line. If a virus or worm floods your site and makes it unavailable, then you are the victim of a denial of service attack.

In a crude sense, repeatedly calling someone on the telephone is a type of denial of service. By calling your victim over and over, you are rendering their phone essentially useless. Methods for dealing with this problem include pleading with the caller to stop, contacting the phone company, or notifying the police. Most of the time, these methods will work for basic telephony, because it's relatively easy to detect the source of crank phone calls.

Unfortunately, this threat is more difficult to defend against on the Internet. Linking IP address information associated with an attack to the true attack source is extremely difficult, due to the ease with which intruders can weave a pattern across the Internet. Furthermore, there is the basic physical principle that if a system can only handle so much capacity, then attackers can simply initiate malicious activity that will exceed that capacity.

How Serious is Cyber Terrorism?

I already know what you're thinking. Cyber security threats don't seem anywhere near as bad as hijacking, truck bombs, and biological weapons. While this may be true, there are two issues that must be considered:

1. All forms of terror can include a cyber component – in fact, some can be directly controlled using computers.
2. Serious inconvenience, disruption, and even misery can be created via cyber attacks.

Most people tend to ignore these issues, perhaps because the effects of cyber security attacks are sometimes less obvious. Here's a story to illustrate: Just after 9/11, I watched live panel discussion on how to prevent future airplane hijacking. One of the experts on the panel endorsed the concept of ground flight control of airplanes to deal with an on-going hijacking. The idea would be that if a plane were hijacked, air traffic control would somehow take over the flight controls and render the hijackers unable to fly the plane from the cockpit.

To my amazement, everyone thought the idea was marvelous, but beyond our technical capacity. I could hardly believe that they were completely ignoring the hacking potential here! Can you imagine the security threats that would emerge if terrorists didn't have to actually get onto planes, but could rather break into ground flight control networks and remotely control the planes from a network? The very idea makes me dizzy.

Calculating Security Risk

With these frightening threats to systems, you might find yourself wondering how suitable protections are identified. You might also recognize the difficulty of countering threats on the inevitable limited budget that organizations and individuals have for cyber security.

For critical infrastructure systems, this is handled through an engineering practice known as risk management. In particular, security professionals measure and manage risk to computer and network infrastructure using a simple equation: They multiply an estimate of the likelihood of an attack by an estimate of the consequences of such attack.

Obviously, this requires some sort of numeric measures to be used as estimates. Perhaps after some consideration, the security engineer might decide that likelihood of attack and consequence of attack would each be given a rating of 3 for high, 2 for medium, and 1 for low. These numbers might seem arbitrary, but when put in use, they help to demonstrate important relationships.

For example, a system with high likelihood and high consequence of attack would have a risk equal to 3 times 3, or 9. If some step is taken to reduce the likelihood of attack from high to medium, then the risk is lowered to 2 times 3, which is 6. Similarly, if the consequences of the attack are lowered, then the risk is lowered as well, and so on.[17]

This notion of risk being proportional to both the likelihood and consequences of attack is fundamental to how we create security defenses. Think about seat belts, for instance: We would never dream of putting a baby into a car seat without buckling, simply because the consequences of an accident are too high for that baby. When adults get into our car, however, we might be more ambivalent about whether they buckle. This is because we measure the consequences as being lower.

I have a friend who was a jeweler in a strip mall in New Jersey. After a long career, he closed his shop, but decided to re-open on a smaller scale in the basement of his home. This introduced some risk problems in his home. First of all, the consequences of a break-in increased dramatically since he was not storing valuables in his home. And second, the likelihood of an attack increased simply because people were now coming into and out of his home, knowing that valuables were present.

In order to better understand the consequences of cyber attack on national infrastructure, let's take a brief look at how cyber terrorism could affect several of major critical system components.

Are the Phones Working?

Many people around the world continue to rely on circuit-switched telephones – the ones that provide only a keypad and receiver. They are connected to copper lines that run out to traditional public switched telephone network lines. You probably do most of your talking on a traditional circuit switched phone in the kitchen of your home.

---

[17] Jon Weiss, now at Lucent, led a group at AT&T in the mid-1980's that invented the use of threat trees to calculate risk based on these equations.

Perhaps more importantly, these phones are typically powered via the trickle of current coming over the phone line. This is critical, because when there is a power outage in an area, it is often the case that people with feature-rich phones requiring power are unable to make calls. Many are forced to use their cell phone, perhaps plugging it into the car for power. In contrast, those with the less feature-rich circuit switched phones are typically unaffected.

I'm not saying that modern telephones are undependable. What I am saying, however, is that we have traded a bit of resiliency in our telephones for the added flexibility that comes with powered devices. Obviously, voice services over the Internet – the familiar VOIP capability so aggressively marketing today – carry this notion to an extreme.

The telecommunications infrastructure in the United States can be grouped specifically into a few basic components: First there are the large transport carrier groups who own miles of underground fiber. These networks support long haul transport of phone calls, data, video, and Internet browsing sessions. Such transport systems are like the super highways in our freeway system – they let you go fast, and they are generally well maintained. But you also need a system of off-ramp highways.

The second component in the American telecommunications infrastructure includes the local phone, cable, and satellite providers, who own the wires connected to buildings and the sides of everyone's garage. These local companies also support voice, data, video, and Internet for customers. They correspond to the local roads and off-ramps in our highway system analogy – they are close to home, tougher to maintain, and don't let you go as fast. Many of these companies are now deploying fiber to the home to increase their ability to sell bundled services.

The third component in our telecommunications infrastructure includes wireless companies. These companies make use of the infrastructure provided by long haul and local providers, but they also operate towers to which you can connect with your cell phone and other wireless devices. The integrity of the connection path between your phone and the nearest tower obviously varies across regions – as you recognize whenever your signal is dying during an important call.

So what are the cyber security risks to telecommunications in the United States? In considering this question, one must recognize that telecommunication networks provide the means over which most cyber attacks are likely to occur. For this reason, many experts posit that a massive cyber attack on any nation would not involve any tampering with basic communications backbones. This would be like destroying the roads before a ground attack.

Keep in mind, however, that if the purpose of a cyber attack is to deny access to landlines, cable television, mobile telephony, pagers, email, Internet access, or even instant messaging, then telecommunications could easily be targeted. For hackers, this could be attractive, if only for the attention such an attack would be given. From the perspective of massive cyber attack to infrastructure, if basic communications are obliterated, the effects on a target nation could be more effective than conventional weapons.

Denial of service is not the only type of threat to national telecommunications systems. We all know that citizens, corporations, and government organizations regularly send and receive valuable information over telephones and computer networks. Such information is obviously much more at risk if someone has managed to infiltrate the telecommunications provider's systems for the purpose of listening. This is certainly unlikely, but must be considered.

During the majority of the past half century, proprietary circuit-switched technology was used for telephone and data connections. This approach proved to be highly reliable in supporting national telecommunications needs, as you probably observed. Furthermore, the limited exposure to the basics of proprietary telecommunications did have a throttling effect on the number and type of attacks that were present.[18]

With the advent of the Internet and its open, non-proprietary services and protocols, however, interesting new opportunities have arisen for hackers. This results in a Catch-22 situation in which our open technology prevents hidden catastrophic vulnerabilities, while at the same time allowing any known vulnerabilities to be known by *everyone*. Think of Internet technology as being in a glass house.

Perhaps more worrisome is the threat that arises when shared telecommunications services are operated across the Internet through collective agreements. The Domain Name System (DNS) and the Border Gateway Protocol (BGP) are two examples of Internet utilities that many experts view as being almost trivial to disrupt. In both cases, individuals groups can inject bogus changes to the Internet infrastructure, with no centralized (or even distributed) police force to stop them.

As you might guess, this produces enormous risk to any telecommunications service that relies on the integrity of the Internet. Email, web services, and any types of electronic commerce rely directly on jointly operated services such as DNS and BGP. The cyber security risk here is considerable, and is poorly understood by policy makers in most countries.

What Happened to the Power?

Human beings are dependent on power – period. Except in the most remote and extreme areas, extended losses of power bring great hardship onto residents and businesses. As such, we must presume that cyber terrorists already understand the target-rich environment that exists in any nation's power systems.

---

[18] Be careful with this point. Security experts refer to this type of protection as "security through obscurity," and it has obvious drawbacks when adversaries do obtain information about a target system or technology.

Power generation systems are, for the most part, either conventional or nuclear. Both involve complex systems that heat water to produce steam. This steam is used to drive turbines that generate electrons onto a massive transport network of power lines. The high voltage electric power carried on these lines is gradually reduced to levels that are safe for distribution into your home and business.

Power systems generate waste, employ large numbers of human beings, include huge physical plants, rely on massive electromechanical systems, and include many, many computers and networks. Such computers and networks are of obvious interest to the cyber attacker, especially where nuclear power and waste products are being generated. Of course, attackers fully understand that you don't just break into a core reactor. A better approach is to target the computer systems that might be connected to, or contain critical information about, a core reactor.

Now, cyber terrorists with a broadband connection cannot cause a Chernobyl-like disaster at your local nuclear power plant. But this does not imply that cyber terrorism is a non-issue for power plants and systems, especially in the United States. In fact, serious national consequences can occur as a result of the dependence of this industry on computer and network systems.

The software, for example, that is embedded in power plants appears to be no more reliable or secure than any other software developed for less critical applications. Recall the scenario mentioned in our first chapter in which the Nuclear Regulatory Commission discovered a safety monitoring computer program with a serious bug. The likelihood that additional bugs might be present in similar software would seem pretty high.

The major power system-related question for most readers is this: Can cyber terrorists shut off the lights in my home? The answer is maybe, but the likelihood improves greatly if cyber terrorism is combined with more conventional terrorist measures. For example, if the objective is to remove power service from a specific region, perhaps by dropping a bomb onto a physical power distribution point, then cyber terrorists might use electronic means to obtain maps of how the distribution is designed.

Terrorists might also try to obtain sensitive information about power system vulnerabilities in a given system, especially if they can place insiders into a target power company. The insider problem is certainly not unique to the power industry, but the consequences of malicious insiders in this industry are obviously considerable.

Where's the Money?

During the morning of 9/11, I stood with so many others on the streets of Washington, DC, watching in horror as a black plume of smoke rose up from the Pentagon. Almost instinctively, I went to an ATM and drew out as much cash as it would give me. Some readers might argue that such action is inappropriate, because it contributes to public panic, and they may be right.

But this does illustrate the importance of financial soundness in times of national stress. If the ATM in Washington had not given me cash on that morning, it would have just made an already horrific day much worse. The story also illustrates the responsibility that the owners and operators of financial services infrastructure have to maintain soundness in their systems and to avoid any types of cyber security catastrophes.

The good news is that considerable emphasis has been directed toward reducing security risks in the financial services industry. This includes the massive investments made by businesses to reduce fraud over the past decades; but it also includes the substantive initiatives being worked across most banks today to protect their computers and networks from hackers, criminals, and cyber terrorists.

One insider problem that banks have seen is the so-called salami attack. This involves repeated theft of small amounts of money. For example, a dishonest clerk might steal a few cents from the travel reimbursements of employees over a large period of time. No single transaction would raise an eyebrow, but in aggregate, the theft can be significant. In the United States, Sarbanes-Oxley controls have reduced the risk of this attack somewhat. But the potential remains.

Banks must also address phishing attacks in which account-related information is stolen from their customers. The theft is done via a familiar, but bogus request that victims supply personal information to avoid some unpleasant or annoying action. Unfortunately, there are no good solutions to the problem currently – and it's only a matter of time before banks being to retreat from their Internet strategies to avoid the risk.

In the mid 1980's, a group of security consultants from AT&T met with system managers from a large investment bank in New York City. The bank apparently was running applications that transferred sizable payments to creditors every Friday afternoon at 3:45 PM. This transfer had to be reliable because late payments carried penalties.

Things worked fine for years, but they suddenly began to notice unexplainable problems with their network just before 3:45 PM every Friday. Everyone suspected insider financial sabotage because the source of the trouble jumped around in a random manner, almost as if to avoid detection. The team tried hard to pinpoint what was going on, but could not obtain accurate evidence.

Ironically, the problem stopped once the consulting group began establishing a more visible presence at the bank. Everyone presumed that the malicious insider probably noticed the ragged-looking security engineers wandering around the trading floor, and just figured that the heat was getting a bit too close. So in the end, the attack stopped.

But this incident left me with an uneasy feeling. The attack, if indeed it really was one, could have targeted great sums of money. Furthermore, the fact that a team of trained forensic security experts could not locate this problem illustrates, in a small way, the potential for a scenario that might have more serious consequences for the financial sector.

Citizens of most companies are totally reliant on computer and network systems for the personal financial needs. Many view access to their money using an ATM machine, for instance, as a basic human right. In addition, businesses obviously rely on the availability of financial systems to support their day-to-day operational needs. Their supply chain management, their point of sale systems, and their advertising and marketing methods are all heavily dependent on computing.

Another point, made resoundingly clear on 9/11, is that the software, computing, and networking infrastructure supporting financial firms are as vital (if not more) to operations as the structural integrity of buildings. Anyone who believes that such cyber infrastructure will not be targeted more aggressively by a future cyber terrorist attack is simply not being realistic.

Furthermore, the customized software powering the financial infrastructure is increasingly developed in non-traditional ways. Much of this software development, for example, is performed in countries for which the link between government and industry is somewhat blurred. This may be fine, but the result is that these countries now have a direct pipeline to the software powering critical financial systems. The presence of such access certainly must be factored into any estimation of national security risk.

Three Thousand Tooth Brushes to Iraq?

Cyber attacks pose an interesting dilemma for the military. Specifically, if a domestic enemy attacks domestic infrastructure, then most countries view this as a law enforcement issue. This complicates how the military deals with cyber security for two reasons:

- Domestic infrastructure attacks could have strategic military importance.

- The geographic location of some attack source is tough to reliably determine.

The military in most countries includes three components. There is a strategic component tasked with the overall planning, architecture, and methodologies to be used in theater and non-theater engagement (a theater is a place where you fight a war). There is also a tactical component, empowered to perform the steps involved in dealing with a real-time situation. And there is the sustaining base component, which involves the systems that allow military organizations to function. This includes payroll systems, families benefits, food preparation, and on and on.

This distinction is important because so often we hear the phrase "hacking the military," without any information about what specifically is being attacked. We presume immediately when we hear such talk that hackers are using computers to run tanks into walls or to cause airplanes to lose contact with the ground. More likely, such cyber attacks generally focus on military Web sites, part of the non-tactical, non-strategic sustaining base.

The military has tried to assess its level of risk over the years through a series of calculated exercises. Back in the late 1990's, several exercises were run in which good guys broke into military computer and network systems. The good-guy attack team showed that by taking their time and avoiding obviously detectable actions, they were able to get through most of the computer network defenses that the military had established.

This is a useful finding, one that all organizations must consider. Specifically, it showed that the most serious cyber attacks will probably not come barreling into an organization's network with guns blazing and rockets firing. No, the cyber terrorist will more likely use the techniques demonstrated in this valuable military exercise: They will proceed slowly with the goal of not being noticed. They will patiently build up enough privileged access to perform the attack only when the time is right.

Of course, the military's cyber attack experience is not confined to exercises. Dorothy Denning of the Naval Postgraduate School relates in her excellent book *Information Warfare and Security* the story of five hackers from the Netherlands who penetrated computer systems at 34 military sites on the Internet, many supporting the 1991 U.S. war against Iraq. A program manager at the Air Force Office of Special Investigations explained at the time that these hackers had so much information and control that "instead of sending bullets to the Gulf, they could have sent toothbrushes." This is obviously unacceptable.

4 Government Issues In Cyber Security

PICTURE THIS. If enemy airplanes suddenly swooped in over your home and started dropping bombs, what would you do? My guess is that you'd rush your spouse and kids to the safest place you could possibly find. You'd stay there until either the bombing stopped or the military intervened.

You would *not*, I'm quite certain, pull out a shoulder-mounted ground-to-air missile launcher from under your bed and start firing back at the planes – at least that seems a normal presumption for the majority of citizens.[19]

This scenario illustrates how responsibility for national protection strategy is divided in most countries:

- Foreign attacks are addressed by the military
- Domestic crimes are addressed by law enforcement
- Minor scuffles are addressed by individuals

---

[19] My friends and associates in Texas love to brag that they may be the exception here.

This approach has been in place for many years, especially in America. Citizens and businesses in the United States simply have not had to deal directly with foreign threats.

People in New Jersey do not, for example, send Grandpa up onto the roof with field glasses to watch for incoming. It just doesn't happen that way, at least, from the perspective of non-cyber related attack. Rather, they rely on a centralized military or law enforcement infrastructure to address broad attacks coming from some powerful external source.

Government Security Responsibility

Cyber security for national infrastructure will require a rethinking of this defensive responsibility scheme. The key issue is that cyber attacks can emanate from sources that are local, remote, domestic, or foreign. They could be launched by an individual or a group. They could be large-scale or specifically focused. They could be part of a benign test, or part of some massive terrorist plot. They could be casual probes from hackers using PCs in their homes, or intense scans from criminal groups.

As a result, it is generally impossible to accurately differentiate between these various attack cases. For example, no organization can install a security device that will examine attacks as they occur, and identify the source and characteristics of the attack. It just doesn't work that way. [20]

It is thus not reasonable to expect any one branch of a national government to accept complete responsibility for cyber security of its critical infrastructure, simply because no government group will ever know which cases are appropriate for national treatment. This is worth repeating:

---

[20] Beware when vendors make this claim. I've seen it in the intrusion detection and now intrusion prevention communities.

It is generally not possible for a government or any other group to determine accurately the true source of a cyber attack.

As a result, it would not make sense for one government agency to focus on hackers, another agency to focus on terrorists, and yet another to focus on foreign cyber wars. They must all be considered jointly, because as we've said, experts involved in even the most mature national cyber security investigations might not be able to tell the difference. This is true for attacks that are in progress, as well as ones that have completed.

The fact that national cyber boundaries are tough to define makes matters more difficult. Unlike with political maps, boundaries in cyberspace are fuzzy at best. Even in those cases where evidence does exist that some cyber attack has crossed the boundaries of different countries, law enforcement response is not always easy.

"The crossing of borders," write Robert Heverly and Morgan Wright in a recent essay on cyberspace law and computer forensics, "complicates investigative efforts as two law enforcement agencies must now act in concert while at the same time observing local laws that may or may not permit the disclosure of identifying information to foreign nationals."

To deal with such ill-defined boundaries, the public sector has no choice but to expand its attention toward private resources, and the private sector must assume a similarly increased role for public resources. The resultant partnership between these sectors must be crafted carefully, because great risk emerges in any infrastructure protection initiatives between government and private groups.

This risk was well-illustrated during World War II when organized crime was enlisted to protect American shipping ports from Nazi saboteurs. The deal was crafted on the observation that mobsters controlled these ports, and could hence police them most effectively. Once the United States government realized, however, that the only real security threat came from the mobsters themselves stealing war supplies, this dubious partnership was ended.[21]

A current construct to enable partnership between public and private sectors involves so-called Information Sharing and Analysis Centers (ISACs). Created during the Clinton Administration, ISACs were designed for critical infrastructure sectors such as information technology, financial services, and telecommunications.

ISAC sector participants, with government involvement, are encouraged to set up shared resources, and to gather together for frequent meetings to share security indicators, explain vulnerabilities, and suggest potential fixes. The motivation for an ISAC is based on the promotion of common national good.

As you might guess, the effectiveness of any ISAC is complicated by normal industrial competition. Suppose, for example, that some bank is hit with security problems and begins to lose customers. Why should another bank provide information through an ISAC to assist the weaker bank in retaining its customer base? Darwin would suggest that the weaker bank with bad security should simply go out of business.

Government Security Requirements

Several years ago, I agreed to review of a set of computer security requirements being developed by a government agency in Washington. I nearly fainted, however, when I saw the enormous size of the two-volume document they sent over. It came in one of those cardboard boxes used to store paper for a copy machine. I tried my best to review the document, but could only get through a tiny fraction.[22] In spite of this, I was still able to generate about a hundred or so detailed comments – mostly criticisms.

---

[21] This theme re-emerges when organizations hire cyber criminals on the premise that they are the only *true* computer security experts.

[22] To be more precise, I spent *exactly* two hours reviewing the document while my students at the Stevens Institute completed their cyber security final exam.

After apologizing to my government contacts for only getting through a small portion of the material, I forgot about the situation until a few months later when I received a letter thanking all of us for our valued participation. I remember seeing dozens of well-known security experts as reviewers on the full list. My heart sank in deep embarrassment at my weak effort. I immediately regretted that I had not spent more hours reviewing the document.

As a courtesy to the reviewers, the government sent us the full slate of comments generated by everyone. Amazingly, I found that my set of comments constituted the *vast majority* of what had been received. Sure, there were one or two other comments that I had not generated, but it was clear that most of the reviewers had sent nothing at all. They had not even bothered to read the thing.

It is therefore instructive to examine the difference between a *good* cyber security requirement and a *bad* one. Briefly put, a good security requirement is clear, concise, tractable, and non-ambiguous. A bad one will ramble on, will express a fuzzy thought, and will often be impossible to implement in a reasonable manner. Furthermore, good security requirements fit together into a cohesive whole, rather than as a collection of unrelated, stand-alone protections. Consider the following example cyber security requirement:

> *All Intranet users must select passwords that are at least eight characters long and that include at least one non-numeric character.*

On the surface, this requirement seems straightforward. It's obviously intended to force users to pick longer and more complex passwords that will be tougher to guess. I've seen variations on this password requirement a thousand times, especially for systems supporting government applications.

The problem, unfortunately, is that writing requirements for information technology and network systems is a difficult task. It's amazingly easy to write requirements that mislead slightly, and leave certain details out that could lead to problems.

Consider, for example, that our example password requirement does not explain what a "user" of the Intranet is. So if you connect your PC to the local Intranet, are you required to use a long and complex password for access to your operating system? Does it mean that any application running on a system resident on the Intranet must enforce passwords accordingly? Can your screen saver password be a short word? Or is this just a requirement on *access* to the Intranet?

I know that this seems like nit-picking, but computer scientists have long since recognized that nit-picking is essential to proper cyber system engineering, especially in security. Little inaccuracies or improperly interpreted statements could easily lead to the type of vulnerabilities that criminals look for. Let's examine another requirement with somewhat different problems:

> *All user activity on the system must be regulated by a segregation of duty policy.*

This requirement is certainly familiar to readers in the United States who are addressing Sarbanes-Oxley regulations, or who have gone through certification and accreditation on certain types of government applications. The seemingly obvious notion here is that no single user should have too much power. For Sarbanes-Oxley, this is supposed to prevent fraud from occurring at the senior executive level (perhaps a dubious claim at best).[23]

The problems here are several. First, if "user" activity includes system administration, then this might be impossible to implement in some settings – especially ones where all-powerful root-type privileges are coded into the environment for administrators and operators. Furthermore, the requirement is absurd in the sense that it requires that *any* segregation of duty policy be present for compliance – even if it is a terrible one!

---

[23] I am unaware of any serious academic study on whether Sarbanes-Oxley controls would have prevented the fraud that destroyed Enron and WorldCom.

Security Policy and the Orange Book

The full set of security requirements that must be enforced in a given environment is called a *security policy*. Without a security policy, an organization's cyber security is like a ship adrift at sea. Even individuals must make security policy decisions about their computing use, albeit under somewhat different circumstance.

A security policy includes all the decisions being made about security in a given environment. If you buy software to restrict the Web sites your children visit on the home computer, then this is part of your family's security policy. If a security executive in some firm decides that employees must be prevented from using evil WiFi, then that decision is part of the firm's security policy. If your company's security team decides that no .zip files are allowed in your email, then that is a security policy decision as well.

Here's a tip: If anyone *ever* asks you how to improve cyber security, an answer that always works under any set of circumstances is this: Improve your security policy. This response works just as well for the technically illiterate as for security professionals. ("In answer to your question about cyber attack risk," replied the handsomely compensated security engineer, "I'd suggest that you improve your security policy.")

Ensuring that a security policy is actually enforced is a difficult matter. In both government and industry, most people view security policies as an unnecessary nuisance. "People form close-knit work groups in which people trust each other," writes security expert Mich Kabay, "they do not lock their desks when they leave them for a few minutes, so why should they obey the network security policy that dictates locking their sessions?"

Suppose, for example, that you ask the participants in some computer and network user community to keep their anti-virus software current. If this security policy requirement dictates that users do anything more than perhaps clicking on something once (maybe twice), then you will see mixed results. Some of the more diligent and technical users will do as you say. But the remainder will ignore the request, citing the impossible hardship of doing what is being required.[24]

One of the earliest and most prominent attempts by government to create a general computer security policy came in the early 1980's. A now-defunct United States government group known as the National Computer Security Center (NCSC) created a framework called the Orange Book (so named for the color of its cover) for defining the security of computer operating systems. A related series of policy books with matching colors was created to enhance the Orange Book. The full set was referred to as the Rainbow Series, and I must say that the colorful spines did look rather nice up there on the shelf.

Perhaps the best aspect of these documents was that they were small and easy to read. Ten minutes spent flipping through the Orange Book gave you a pretty good idea of what was inside. Managers, engineers, programmers, and system administrators thus had a common language that could be used to talk about security policy. That was a huge advantage. People could actually communicate with each other about security.

The way the security policy framework worked in the Orange Book was as follows: A "grade" would be issued for the security of some new or existing system. If a given system had ample provision for security – as defined by the specific security requirements in the Orange Book – then it would be given a good grade. Conversely, if the system had poor security functionality, then it would be given a bad grade. A team from the NCSC would serve as auditors, and would spend considerable time studying the system under evaluation carefully.

In spite of the fact that everyone constantly fought over whether the Orange Book included the right requirements, the document and associated processes worked pretty well. In fact, the Orange Book

---

[24] My favorite excuse came from an executive who complained that passwords on Blackberry devices make it tough to send email while driving. (*Gulp.*)

dominated computer security policy work for the decade of the 1980's and well into the 1990's. I spent nearly half a decade myself working on a Unix system at AT&T that was targeted at receiving one of the Orange Book ratings.[25] I still think that Unix system, now twenty years old, was superior in the security sense, to most of the operating systems in use today.

The Orange Book is now long forgotten as a useful tool. I believe this is due primarily to the economic pressures exerted by the Internet and the World Wide Web. That is, when the Web emerged, considerable attention was diverted from good security toward rapidly executable business models for on-line products. NCSC certification took too long, perhaps years to complete – and from 1995 until about 2000, everyone was in a terrible rush to make money.

Happily, the Orange Book did spur on a series of additional efforts at defining security policies. The Canadians, for example, created a larger set of criteria than the original Orange Book, choosing to include requirements for denial of service, among other things. Other international groups followed suit with their own sets of security criteria, albeit with ever-increasing complexity.

Most recently, a policy framework known as the Common Criteria has been used occasionally for specifying computer security policy requirements in government systems. It is a reasonable framework, with elements that include an activity that looks like some sort of self-certification. I think this is a good idea, since external evaluation is so error prone and subject to misinterpretation.

But the Common Criteria is still too complicated. I've been in information security for two decades, and after multiple briefings, demonstrations, and even courses on the Common Criteria, I'm still not certain that I could offer a very good explanation of what it entails. (This statement will, no doubt, lead to dozens of marketing

---

[25] The system, called Unix System V/MLS, was targeted at the Orange Book B1 level. Chuck Flink, then of AT&T Labs, was the chief designer.

emails in my in-box with offers to properly explain the Common Criteria – for a modest fee, of course.)

Government's Cryptographic Puzzle

Let me explain, in a nutshell, the problem that most national governments have been trying to solve with respect to the encryption and decryption of information in cyberspace:

Traditionally, government has used physical surveillance and wiretaps to catch criminals and terrorists. A typical illustration might involve two wise guys – perhaps John and Sammy – talking on the phone. Law enforcement listens to their conversation via wiretap, and when something is said that implicates them in some crime, an arrest is made. Using this approach, law enforcement has had good success. Most honest citizens are grateful that such methods are in use.

The problem that arises in more modern contexts is that instead of using open, unencrypted telephones, wise guys might now use some sort of encrypted communications, probably over an Internet protocol-based network. If the encryption being used is weak, then law enforcement *might* be able to decipher the discussion if they can capture the right packets, and break the weak code.

This explains, by the way, why the FBI and others have lobbied long and hard to control the propagation of *really strong* encryption technology. Such lobbying has sparked a huge debate as to the relative merits of cryptography in society. Some say it should be controlled, whereas others say it should be allowed without any sort of regulation. Participants on both sides of the argument are equally passionate in their beliefs.

"All technologies – cryptography included – can be used for good or for ill," writes the chairman of a National Resarch Council committee studying cryptography's role in society. "They can be used to serve society or to harm it, and cryptography will no doubt be used for both purposes by different groups."

Cryptography containment initiatives led by government advocates have not been popular to date. Most citizens have tended to dislike the notion that government can somehow tap into their Internet activity. Businesses, on the other hand, generally oppose cryptography containment measures because it prevents the use of these methods to protect information and remain competitive. When the government of a nation tries to limit such use, they place their business community at a global disadvantage.

The important National Research Council committee mentioned above had this to say about ever-evolving proposals for national containment strategies of cryptography: "Export controls on products with encryption capabilities are a compromise between the needs of national security to conduct signals intelligence and the needs of US and foreign businesses operating abroad to protect information."

So, what is a government to do? It has become patently obvious that limiting the growth, propagation, and proliferation of encryption technologies is close to impossible. Anyone in virtually any country can design and build cryptographic methods, and they are doing so. This is not nuclear weaponry we're talking about. It's much less complicated, and its use has exploded.

My belief is that law enforcement should focus on the end-points of a conversation as a better means for catching criminals. Keep in mind that encrypted information *eventually* must be decrypted to be useful. Thus, instead of trying to listen to the encrypted communication link between John and Sammy, law enforcement could use *deception* to spoof the identity of the end-points, which is, of course, exactly how criminals such as pedophiles are caught on the Internet.

Furthermore, rather than focusing on encryption as a tool for the enemy, government must come to recognize its amazing significance as a means for coordinating homeland cyber security defense strategies between government and industry. We know that for any homeland cyber security protection initiatives to really work, secure, underlying frameworks for coordinated activity are required. Cryptography will enable such secure collaboration.

I once heard Jim Reeds from Bell Labs relate that law enforcement in the United States was originally opposed to the use of radio when it was first invented. They apparently cited security concerns, and predicted that criminals would dominate the use of radios. That argument seems so ridiculous now when you think about which group uses radio more than anyone else. The answer, of course, is law enforcement.

In the end, the primary storyline associated with government use of cryptography will not be around the containment and export control of encryption technology and algorithms. It will be instead on the use of encryption technology to accomplish government's mission. The sooner all parties recognize this seemingly inevitable conclusion, the better.

US National Cyber Security Strategy

If you ask any American about our national strategy for protection of our homeland, the discussion inevitably turns to the ever-present alert levels and their associated colors.

Every day, the people who are in charge of our nation's homeland security declare a security alert level – presumably, to help Americans understand the degree of risk that exists on that given day. It's not unlike the Smokey the Bear signs advertising fire risk outside our nation's parks. In both the homeland security and Smokey the Bear systems, indicators are examined and used to decide what an appropriate quantification of risk might be.

The result – as we all know – is a daily alert status in which we are told that the nation is vigilant to one of the following levels: Low, Guarded, Escalated, High, and Severe. Most Americans, if asked, have absolutely no concept of how such alert status reporting should influence their lives. In fact, people are often rather cynical when it comes to the alert status.

"So ... does this mean that I *should* or *should not* get on the plane?" people ask sarcastically any time the alert level is raised. "Do I cancel my trip to New York or not?"[26]

Homeland security leaders respond to such inquiries in a fairly predictable manner: *Yes*, they reply, we should all continue doing exactly as we've always done. So, *yes*, get on the plane and *yes*, go to New York. But they add that we should be much more vigilant, generally omitting details on what that means exactly.

Before we discount vague security guidance, we shouldn't forget that criminals have been caught after being featured on television episodes of *America's Most Wanted*. Sure, such programs provide specific information – descriptions, locations, time, crime committed, and so on. This does, however, suggest that asking Americans to be more vigilant can be quite powerful. So let's not be too cynical.

Many people do not realize that we have had a national strategy for protecting cyberspace for some time. It was developed several years ago in the office of the President's former cyber security advisor – Richard Clarke. More recently, the implementation of the national cyber security strategy has fallen into the hands of the Department of Homeland Security. They have since reported on various cyber security objectives, and have even made substantive efforts at elevating the priority given to this post.

The remainder of this chapter will examine the five basic strategic elements of this national cyber security strategy. The strategy is a fine start at defining security protections. It contains excellent recommendations that should be initiated at once. Furthermore, the strategy addresses this complex issue better than one might have ever expected. It does, however, contain flaws.

---

[26] In fairness, color codes have been significantly de-emphasized recently by Homeland Security.

Priority 1: National Cyberspace Security Response System

The United States national cyber security strategy starts with the desire for a large-scale cyberspace security *response* system. This is not unexpected since all security disciplines include response as a key strategic element.

A national cyber response system would include the people, infrastructure, technology, tools, and processes required to detect and react to cyber security problems aimed at American critical infrastructure. Such a system is akin to an active and alert fire department, police department, and emergency squad, ready and waiting to provide assistance to the computers and networks that power critical systems.

An actual response must, by definition, be triggered by some event or indicator. Information must flow to a national collection system, so that appropriate mitigation steps can be performed. Your local ambulance team follows the same process – albeit in a more limited context. Someone falls down, a call is made to a dispatching system, and emergency medical technicians are sent to the victims. Computer scientists refer to this process of handling real time problems as *incident* response.

As mentioned earlier, during the Millennium change, my team at AT&T worked with the White House to establish a response center in Washington. This center served as a centralized means for Y2K-related information to be collected, correlated, and fused into intelligence for the President. Luckily, the Y2K event was largely a non-event and no serious response activities were required. But this center was similar to the response system that homeland security leaders want for America.

Building and operating a national security response center is a complicated task. A key issue in such a center involves security threshold triggers. Like the nuclear silo operator with his hand quivering over the red button, the operators of any national security incident response center will have to determine when some event is significant enough to require response. They'll need to make decisions based on imperfect models of what actually constitutes an attack.

Let's illustrate security response using a whimsical, non-computing example: Suppose, for the sake of illustration, that you've just bought yourself a brand new home, and you step out onto the front porch to have a look at your new neighborhood. You happen to notice that a long black car has just stopped in front of your home. The rear window comes down and someone in the back seat peers out at you suspiciously through dark sunglasses.

Question: Would you call the police?

Assuming you would not, you simply stare back, and after a moment, the window goes up and the car pulls away. Now, in my travels around the world posing this scenario, I've never found anyone who really *would* call the police at this point. There simply is not enough evidence that a real attack is underway. ("Yes, officer, the car slowed down and they looked at me ... hello, *officer?*")

An obvious exception, however, occurs if you've already been on the lookout for such a thing, perhaps as a result of some tip-off from the local police. This is why a national incident response center must maintain accurate real-time intelligence at all times. As events are observed, response analysts can thus *correlate* observed activity with available intelligence.

Let's continue. Suppose now, that after a couple of minutes, you notice the same car returning from the opposite direction. Just as before, it stops in front of your home, but this time both the front *and* rear windows go down, and two heads peer out at you through dark sunglasses. Then, after a moment, both windows go up and the car pulls away mysteriously.

Question: Do you now call the police?

Let's assume that you would not call the police, choosing instead to just go inside the house. But now, after a few minutes, you glance out the window and notice that the car in question is parked in front of your home. The two men, last seen peering at you suspiciously, are now walking up the driveway. Both are wearing threatening looking trench coats. One is carrying a violin case. *Gulp.*

What do you do now? (By the way, when I ask this question to Americans living in Virginia and points south, they all respond that they would be out on the porch shooting – and I don't mean with a camera.) Anyway, if you're like most people, you are now really starting to organize the chain of events in your mind. The process of correlation continues – perhaps instinctively – as you try to make sense of these events.

If you *do* decide to call the police, my guess is that they probably wouldn't be terribly sympathetic with your situation at this point. The only information you have is that a couple of weird guys have driven by your home twice and they're now walking up the driveway. "Maybe you should just calm down and answer the door," is what the police officer would probably tell you, perhaps with a tremendous smirk.

But, of course, the police officer could be wrong.

Maybe what you're seeing actually correlates with some other truly relevant piece of frightening data. Maybe these guys are in the process of coming up your driveway to do something really, really bad. Wouldn't it be a shame if they did and the police officer had ignored your call for assistance? Wouldn't that be exactly the sort of scenario that American government was criticized for allowing during the period before September 11th?

Establishing a national response center requires three basic steps to be completed successfully: First, a center must be created with the ability to actually detect what is going on. Since, as we outlined earlier, the majority of critical infrastructure is owned privately, the detection of attack-related information will have to be done largely by companies and citizens. They will need to be shown how to do this, since most companies have no clue when it comes to detection of security-relevant activity.

Second, the national response center will require access to the best possible intelligence. In the United States, such access is limited by the strict separation enforced between the intelligence community and law enforcement. For example, security compartmentalization laws govern how classified information can be shared. Law enforcement officials cannot be easily briefed on national security-related information unless the proper clearances are held. Making matters even worse, commercial intelligence is not easily co-mingled together among competing businesses.

The third step toward a working national response center includes building some method of actually *responding* to events. Response comes in three flavors: You might make suggestions to your constituency – "It would be nice if you could all go patch your systems." Alternatively, you might just *demand* that some action be taken – "If you don't patch your system, then I will raise your taxes." Or, finally, you could just take the required action on behalf of your constituency – "We have just taken the liberty of remotely accessing and patching your system for you." All of these choices have their respective upsides and downsides.

The bottom line is that the hurdles in doing a national cyber response center are large, but not insurmountable. It is the opinion here that attempting to build such a center is a good idea, and that serious plans should be put in place at once.

Priority 2: National Cyberspace Security Threat and Vulnerability Reduction Program

The second priority in the American national cyber security strategy focuses on the vulnerabilities that exist in national infrastructure. This includes the vulnerabilities one would find in the software, applications, operating systems, networks, and embedded components that power critical systems.

The national strategy focuses on three approaches to dealing with cyber security vulnerabilities in national infrastructure: First, the strategy recommends serious penalties for people who exploit security problems in critical infrastructure. Second, the strategy suggests that all vulnerabilities in critical infrastructure must be identified and removed. Third, the strategy recommends increased emphasis on preventing cyber security vulnerabilities from being introduced into critical systems in the first place.

From the perspective of logical completeness, these three strategy elements would seem appropriate. Stiff penalties can and should be put in place to punish cyber criminals and terrorists, especially if they damage important national infrastructure. Furthermore, identifying, removing, and preventing cyber security vulnerabilities from our key cyber assets are familiar objectives that no one could argue with.

But things are not so simple. To effectively deal with cyber security vulnerabilities in some national infrastructure component, the following conditions must be present:

- The vulnerability must be identifiable.
- Means must exist to reduce the associated risk.
- Motivation must exist to prompt action.

Let's examine each point in turn. First of all, you should know that it is impossible to identify *all* of the vulnerabilities in current operating systems and applications because the software is too complex. Fifty experienced computer scientists with ten million dollars could not do it for the word processing software on your home computer. So, imagine how unlikely it would be to perform this for the millions of lines of software running national infrastructure components.[27]

---

[27] Important point: Remember that it is quite easy to find one or more vulnerabilities, especially if you're not picky about what you find. The challenge is finding and removing *all* of the problems.

As a result, no nation could expect to meet the objective of identifying all of the vulnerabilities in its critical systems. Perhaps a percentage of vulnerabilities could be identified through testing, reviews, and usage, but this would correspond to a different strategic objective – one more along the lines of risk reduction, rather than risk removal.

Regarding the second issue of punishing cyber criminals and terrorists, things would appear on the surface to be somewhat more tractable. For example, if someone is caught damaging a critical infrastructure component in some national asset, then shouldn't that person be punished? Shouldn't serious action be taken to keep that person away from computers and networks?

It's so tempting to agree with this statement, but one must be very careful. Everything is linked together in cyberspace, so damage to some seemingly isolated component could easily be interpreted as having much broader implications. This could result in unfortunate consequences, especially in cases where it is difficult to differentiate an intentional act from an innocent error.

Here's an example: Suppose an administrator from a small Internet service provider accidentally advertises an erroneous network route during routine system chores. This is surprisingly easy to do, and it happens all the time. If this action corrupts routing to a critical infrastructure network, then how would law enforcement know if it was done accidentally or intentionally? Should this person be punished? Should this person be put in jail? And who is to say that law enforcement in some country is in the best position to make this call?

On the third issue of preventing vulnerabilities from finding their way into new systems, I am somewhat optimistic from an engineering perspective. Here's why: We know from years of experience in the computer security community that it is possible to create secure, vulnerability-free code. Computer scientists have demonstrated that tiny pieces of code can be worked over sufficiently to demonstrate correctness. The requirement, however, is that the code must be small, clean, and simple.

For this to happen, software makers need incentives to build smaller, less feature-rich products. Buyers will have to be willing to pay more money for fewer features. To that end, it should be in any national strategy to create economic or regulatory incentives for software makers to simplify their systems. Nothing the government could do in the area of cyber security protection would be more valuable than this. Let me repeat this:

> *The most valuable contribution government can make to cyber security involves providing incentives for software makers to create more correct code.*

Such action on the part of government would greatly ease the cyber security threat across the board. If you asked me when this should occur, I would glance at my watch, check the time, and tell you yesterday.

Priority 3: A National Cyberspace Security Awareness and Training Program

The third national priority involves training and awareness programs to inform citizens and businesses on the issues related to cyber security. This would seem harmless enough, but the truth is that our expectation should be somewhat limited in terms of the real benefits that such training will produce in security posture.

Let's examine this conundrum using one of the most familiar training and awareness cases in recent history: Wearing safety belts in cars. Everyone knows that wearing a safety belt dramatically increases one's chances of avoiding death or serious injury in a car crash. Few awareness campaigns have provided more compelling evidence of major benefit, with only minor inconveniences. You'd think this would be enough.

Indeed, the National Safety Council recently measured safety belt usage in America at 75%. That's good news, because it shows that the vast majority of Americans do buckle up when they get into a car. Furthermore, it's tough to find a six-year-old who will not complain loudly if you forget the buckle them before starting the car. But the "glass is half empty" side of this result is that one out of every four drivers still does *not* wear a safety belt. (Any security officer will tell you that one out of four violations of any security rule will get you fired every time.)

Howard Schmidt, former chairman of the President's Critical Infrastructure Protection Board, referred to safety belts at a recent meeting in New York. "People used to avoid wearing seat belts at all costs, even by snapping the belt shut behind them," he joked. "And then would sit there on that seat belt lump."

Smoking prevention campaigns in the United States are as intense as safety belt campaigns. For decades now, major training efforts have been designed to explain the terrible effects of smoking on health. Strikingly, these campaigns have measured similar results as for safety belts. According to some estimates, almost a quarter of Americans smoke.

It would seem preposterous to believe that a massive training and awareness campaign could ever be created that would stop cyber security problems. Such a program would have to explain to citizens how to avoid clicking on phishing emails, how to properly run anti-virus software, how to run a personal firewall, and on and on. Apart from the non-obvious benefits to citizens and businesses, the inconveniences associated with these actions are considerable.

Here's another training and awareness challenge: For cyber security initiatives to work, you cannot have any exceptions. This is somewhat counter-intuitive, but the truth is that even a small percentage of users ignoring some rule can place an entire infrastructure at risk.

As an example, the domain controllers running on the corporate Intranet at AT&T were recently experiencing an overload, and were causing performance problems in the enterprise. Forensic investigation uncovered a new strain of virus on a tiny percentage of our computers – just a handful of systems. This small number of systems was trying to communicate repeatedly with the controllers on the corporate enterprise, and the impact was widespread.

So what is a nation to do? Certainly, security training and awareness programs should not be scrapped. Any reasonable person would agree that improving compliance with security policy requirements is better than nothing. But perhaps a more reasonable goal would be to focus the awareness programs on those individuals who might have a more profound impact on cyber security than the normal citizen. Perhaps the *purveyors* of critical national infrastructure should be the ones for which training is targeted. This suggestion is important enough, that it should be repeated:

Nations should focus their cyber security training on those who operate their critical infrastructure, rather than on normal citizens.

Emphasizing high-end security training to the administrators and operators of critical systems could produce dramatic results. The effects of operator behavior on critical systems have an obvious multiplier effect. Furthermore, there are fewer people entrusted with this responsibility, so the likelihood of success is greater. As such, national training programs should be created with precisely this focused emphasis.

In fact, anyone working on critical government or national infrastructure systems should be required to demonstrate some reasonable level of training and awareness on cyber security. This could be administered privately or as part of a government initiative. Such focusing training would have a meaningful impact on the security posture of national infrastructure.

Priority 4: Securing Government's Cyberspace

The fourth priority involves the rational goal of improving the security of government cyber infrastructure. It is hard to find any fault with this security goal, especially at a time when audits by groups such as the Government Accounting Office (GAO) are regularly assigning failing grades for information security to federal agencies.

Simply stated, government should lead by example in the cyber security realm through immediate and direct action. For instance, when computer or network systems are bought for federal, state, or local use, proper cyber security protections should be considered paramount in the procurement requirements. This straightforward action has the benefit of requiring no regulation or financial incentives. Rather, by simply emphasizing security requirements in procurement, benefits accrue due to the enormous buying power of the government.

This can only work, obviously, if government procurement processes are well coordinated. Otherwise, security emphasis will vary from one procurement initiative to another, and the desired effect on the marketplace will be more limited. It also requires greater cooperation on security initiatives between federal, state, and local governments. None of this is easy, but the cyber security benefits could be significant.

The specific types of requirements that should be emphasized by government include the following: First, government should demand that no exploitable bugs be present in software that it buys and uses. Almost no single constituency or sector, other than the United States Federal Government, has enough power to make such an initiative succeed. Business, citizens, and the international community would benefit as well, since everyone buys from the same software base.

A second requirement would involve a push toward simplification. Government networks and systems have grown too complex, and as such, they have become difficult to protect. Simplification would require turning off unneeded functionality, removing extraneous components, disabling improper network connections, removing unwanted software, and so on.

As an example of the complexity growth in government networking, my group was doing security work for a major civilian government agency a few years ago. They had complained to us that packets from their network had been found by network operators on the Internet. (Yes, they could have been spoofed, but that's not the point.) Anyway, as their network provider, we were implicated as the most likely source of such spillage, and the customer demanded action.

We immediately tried to determine where these packets could be coming from. A couple of day's worth of scanning and investigation showed that this agency's network was far too complicated. As a result, they had several Internet gateways that were completely unprotected. They also had non-inventoried routers and a lack of controls on remote access. Needless to say, it was amazing that any packets managed to stay in!

Priority 5: International Cyberspace Security Cooperation

This fifth priority in the national strategy – cooperating on cyber security initiatives internationally – may be the toughest of them all. Here are some of the factors that complicate any sort of international cyber security initiatives:

First of all, it is virtually impossible to define a national cyberspace border. Every individual, business, and government in every country in the world must share certain services and resources across borders on the Internet. No one county – and yes, that includes the United States – can claim complete ownership of any aspect of the global cyberspace infrastructure.

Consider, for example, that every Internet-connected device in every country depends on the large distributed database system we know as the Domain Name System (DNS). As we've mentioned earlier, this is the database that maps an Internet address to a more human readable name like yourserver.com or myserver.net. Obviously, any national critical infrastructure depends on this decentralized, global database system being correct.

The DNS operates through a loosely defined administrative protocol that permits people all over the world to make mistakes (ahem) that could introduce problems. Someone in Australia, for example, could easily cause nightmares for an Internet Service Provider in America by improperly advertising incorrect information for a particular domain or address. Even if the Federal Government of the United States wrote stiff laws to improve the robustness of this service, it would not be enforceable on a global scale.

Here's another issue: Cyber attackers love to weave an obscure pattern of network connections behind their activity. The resultant trail of connections between computers and networks is generally so complex that tracing the true identity of the attacker becomes extremely difficult. In many countries, especially in the Far East, policies for sharing traceability information are still, shall we say, evolving. For true international cooperation to exist in cyberspace, a standard must be created for how and when this information is shared during an attack.

What's missing in all these complications is some suitably obvious forum for finding effective international security solutions. In the past, computer scientists have relied most heavily on professional societies such as the IEEE (Institute for Electrical and Electronic Engineers) to drive certain technical standards. The ITU (International Telecommunication Union) has also done good work, but it's been focused on the telecommunications industry.

Perhaps part of the American national strategy should be a more deliberate roadmap for how new and emerging international standards groups should address cyber security. It should be inclusive of law enforcement in different countries, global businesses with infrastructure that might span across dozens of countries, and all the rest of us who simply want to see a more secure globe.

5 Cyber Security Vulnerabilities

L ET US RETURN TO OUR BRIDGE ANALOGY. Consider the following: Suppose that you happen to drive your car up to a large suspension bridge that has the following obvious engineering and safety problems:

- The steel, cabling, and concrete used to construct the bridge riddled with structural flaws.

- Engineers have concluded that the bridge could fall down if these flawed components are not patched quickly.

- The surface of the bridge is seriously impaired and the required sometimes actually weaken the overall structure.[28]

- Bridge operators utilize notification system that provides real-time information about any bridges that might be falling down.

Given this scenario, I would ask whether you would consider actually driving onto this bridge? I've asked this question to many people around the world, and the resounding answer I hear is *no way*. Not a chance. Everyone seems in perfect agreement.

If this is true, then why don't we have a similar opinion for the software that powers our critical infrastructure? After all, the

---

[28] Security administrators are well aware of the new troubles that patches can cause to systems that are at least exhibiting acceptable behavior.

conditions outlined above are certainly present in the global software infrastructure. We all know that software is riddled with flaws, patches sometimes do cause more harm than good, and security experts do deal with these vulnerabilities through a notification system. So why don't people drive up to cyber controlled critical infrastructure and say no?

The answer is simple: Few people envision critical infrastructure in this manner. Most citizens do not consider what might happen to power systems, or to water systems, or to communications as a result of cyber attack. They do not understand the vulnerabilities that can be exploited to make these things happen. They simply assume that these services will be present to support normal day-to-day activities.

Vulnerabilities in Software

Here is what some experts have to say about software and the associated programming profession:

- From Matthew Blaze, world-renowned security guru: "Everybody knows that nobody knows how to write software."

- From Winn Schwartau, author of the book *Information Warfare*, "The bottom line is that it's impossible to test software thoroughly enough to make sure it works all of the time."

- From Fred Brooks Jr., author of the classic book, *The Mythical Man-Month*: "The tar pit of software engineering will continue to be sticky for a long time to come."

So how did our software become so riddled with bugs, errors, and security vulnerabilities? How can an admired profession continue to produce products that cause so many security problems? How can professionals who develop software possibly bear to live with such a situation? Let's address these questions by first examining the identity crisis that exists for professional programmers.

Programmer as Artist: Some programmers claim to create software from pure inspiration, an approach that they claim works best if one has a diverse background in art, music, language, history, and literature. I was recently visiting software companies in California when I ran into a group of programmers of this type. One claimed to me that his classical music training and background provided a great base on which to build creativity in programming.[29]

Programmer as Craftsperson: Some programmers describe their profession in the context of their tools. Their skills are honed under the tutelage of an experienced craftsperson. Dennis Ritchie, one of the co-developers of Unix at Bell Labs, exemplified this view. He said this about the origin of the Unix operating system: "What we wanted to preserve was not just a good environment in which to do programming, but a system around which a fellowship could form."

Programmer as Scientist: Some programmers view their profession as part of a rigorous mathematical discipline. The late Edsger Dijkstra is the patron saint here. He suggested treating computer programs as mathematical objects and to use proofs of theorems about these objects to demonstrate correctness. The primary argument against this scientific approach is its difficulty for non-experts.

Programmer as Businessperson: Some businesspeople consider programming as an extension of how they describe organizational processes. The tool of choice here is the awkward English language-like COBOL language, designed when Dwight Eisenhower was President. Here's a gem from Professor Dijkstra: "The use of COBOL cripples the mind; its teaching should, therefore, be regarded as a criminal offense."

Programmer as Engineer: Some programmers view their profession as involving construction of large programs by multi-person teams. Engineers create requirements, construct designs, and code systems using structural methods. Unfortunately, as evidenced by the plethora

---

[29] The next time you're about to go under the knife in an operating room, I'll bet you'd like to hear that your surgeon was trained primarily as a musician.

of problems we've cited throughout this text, software engineering methodologies have not been successful in preventing vulnerabilities from creeping into code.

By the way, the Internet boom era did little to ease this identity crisis for programmers. The pressure to rush software to market was no longer just driven by impatient customers. The World Wide Web fueled a vicious race to become the fastest to do virtually anything. This fury to make money through rapid product deployment found its way into virtually every aspect of software development. The result was more bad software and more identity confusion for programmers.

As an example, during the height of the Internet bubble, I had a graduate student enrolled in my course on computer security at the Stevens Institute of Technology who handed in an assignment with a legal disclaimer. I came to understand that his immature concept, which was riddled with software design problems and obvious vulnerabilities, apparently had venture funds lined up. (I signed the disclaimer, and gave him a B-minus.)

I can state with confidence that in nearly two decades as a computer scientist, I've never seen a piece of non-trivial software that worked properly in all possible cases. Let me be clear: This does not imply that software fails in all cases. Most software, in fact, muddles along in a reasonably acceptable manner. For example, I'm using software to write this book that is fine for general use, most of the time. But on occasion, it crashes.

How does software correctness influence the safety and security of our critical infrastructure elements? The sad answer is that flaws in software can allow wide open doors for malicious intruders. This is a foundational notion, so let's highlight it:

Flaws in software can allow wide open doors for malicious intruders.

In business settings, programming errors introduce vulnerabilities that allow malicious entry into applications, operating systems, and network elements. The Computer Emergency Response Team Coordination Center (CERT/CC) at Carnegie-Mellon University produces streams of such advisories for organizational use. In 1995, they reported on 171 software vulnerabilities, which is roughly one every other day. That might sound like a lot until you hear that over four *thousand* were reported in 2002.[30]

The implications for national critical infrastructure are obvious. In particular, for any nation to become sufficiently secure from cyber attack, it will need to adopt a national approach to dealing with software correctness. Every nation must increase research investment in the areas of software correctness techniques, and must improve incentives for software developers to create less complicated code.

It's fashionable in some circles to suggest that lawyers might lead the way in this push toward fewer software vulnerabilities. Some like to suggest that if a serious cyber catastrophe were to occur, the resultant lawsuits would be the only way to get the profession back on track. I personally do not agree with this view. The secret to fixing software lies instead in the following urgent actions:

Professional View. Leaders in the software profession – computing academics, software executives, government officials, and technical society officers – must first address the identity crisis in software. They must collectively arrive at a more uniform view of programming that combines scientific rigor and artistic creativity, with the proper use of tools and methodologies. This effort should be managed as a Manhattan Project to save the software profession.

Simpler Software. The software process and the associated features embedded in software must be simplified. In companies, software features must be booked as *liabilities*, and lines of code as costs. Chief Information Officers could be the change agents for simplification of software. Companies and projects should be funded to develop software with fewer features. Economy of design should be the rallying cry across the software community. Buyers of software should be willing to pay more money for simplified functionality.

---

[30] Things are so crazy now, that they don't even bother reporting such statistics.

Procurement and Maintenance: Executives who buy software should begin to examine the financial burden of patching broken products. Contracts might begin to stipulate that "buyer-beware" is no longer acceptable.[31] Remember: For thousands of years, the sale of any types of goods and services has worked this way. Finding creative ways to stand behind one's product is one of the underlying pillars of free enterprise. The software industry should be no different.

Software Maintenance

It should be obvious to you that software does not *wear out*. The zeros and ones in a computer program will remain intact from now until the end of eternity. So you'd think that this maintenance-free aspect would make software one of the most resilient products imaginable. Sadly, this is not the case, and the industry has developed the curious notion of software maintenance for a product that remains intact forever.

In particular, the maintenance of software involves dealing with the constant changes that occur around it use. Here are some examples of this evolution:

- User expectations for software change

- Underlying computer hardware evolves

- Network capacity and connectivity options grow

- New software features emerge that users want

None of these changes are problematic, because they all lead to an improved software product.

Maintenance driven by requirements evolution is thus appropriate, and carries no inherent security vulnerabilities. The process involves installing new code, updating aspects of the code, and even throwing out old code for new. Obviously, some types of

---

[31] Here's an idea: Start a company that refunds your money if the software is defective. Imagine how tentative you'd be on the introduction of new features.

software maintenance are more challenging than others. Ones involving larger systems, especially if they include embedded hardware, are generally more complex than any other.

For example, it is difficult to swap new software in and out of big embedded systems like the Space Shuttle.[32] The software in this type of complex spacecraft is tightly integrated with its hardware. As such, new features that are required must be integrated carefully, often using hardware simulators. The result is a complex software maintenance challenge, but again, this is perfectly reasonable from a security perspective.

A far less reasonable and more degrading aspect of software maintenance involves dealing with the constant stream of software vulnerabilities, errors, and bugs in our software. The resultant maintenance process is unpredictable, expensive, and inefficient.

"The average customer of the computing industry," writes Edsger Dijkstra in his book, *Selected Writings on Computing*, "has been served so poorly that he expects his system to crash all the time, and we witness a worldwide distribution of bug-ridden software for which we should be deeply ashamed."

So what is the security problem here? We know that cyber terrorists can exploit vulnerabilities to attack infrastructure. If the last line of defense in avoiding such exploitation is the software maintenance process known as patching, then we are all in big trouble. Here are some reasons why:

First of all, software patches do not always work. In fact, sometimes the patches themselves introduce problems such as memory leaks or application breakage, previously not found in the software. In these cases, we have the classic "medicine-worse-than-the-disease" syndrome.

In addition, scheduling problems could emerge in some forms of software patching, particularly in an enterprise. Specifically, if a patch

---

[32] My first job in the 1980's involved developing inertial measurement software for the mechanical gyros that were in the Space Shuttle at the time.

is being applied to a system with complex business applications running, then the test process could be long and cumbersome. This could lead to the absurd situation in which your system becomes out of date for new patches, while you're off testing and installing old patches.

After the Slammer worm incident of 2003, many security administrators were criticized for not installing the proper patch in advance of the worm. Their rationale was that they were waiting for an upcoming service pack from Microsoft, which would have rolled in the patch and saved a fair amount of work. This is a reasonable view, but one that no security administrator would dare hold today.

A simple analysis suggests that a large organization could easily spend a million dollars a month patching its software. Suppose there are, say, fifty thousand desktops in some organization, and that forty-five thousand are patched centrally. This is how almost every company on earth does it, and we will assume that this centralized patching costs the company basically zero.[33]

But the remaining five thousand systems are owned by people such as developers and researchers who cannot be managed centrally. Their specialized work requires that they control all aspects of their desktop, so they must patch themselves, with some assistance from an internal software vulnerability reporting service.

This interaction requires that each developer and researcher review and try to understand all reported patches, install and test the ones that are deemed applicable, troubleshoot any side-effects that might occur on their desktop applications, reboot their systems if necessary, and refer trouble to a help desk if all else fails.

Surveys might thus suggest that for this population about two hours per month are spent on these activities. So, for five thousand people, that about ten thousand hours per month, which is probably

---

[33] We all know that patches do not always install properly, sometimes break applications, often introduce user or administrator confusion, can slow down processing, and on and on. These have financial impact, but since accurate cost measurements are not easy to create, we'll stick with the zero cost estimate.

around a million dollars of costs per month. This does not include patching costs for servers, routers, and network elements that are usually patched on a regular basis.

Imagine this: If software was correct in the first place, these costs would not exist. All of the time and energy expended could be redirected toward delighting customers and shareholders. In fact, if you tally the patching costs for every sector of every industry in every country, the global dividends of having correct software could easily reach into the many, many billions of dollars – *monthly*!

System Administration

System administration involves the daily care and feeding of a computer. On your home system, it involves installing software, arranging your desktop, setting up WiFi, and other related tasks. In a network environment, it involves configuring routers, troubleshooting switching problems, administering servers, and so on.

From a security perspective, administration involves the steps required to keep intruders away from your system. On your home machine, this usually means trying to keep viruses, Spam, spyware, and other forms of malware from entering via your network connection. It may also mean, however, policing the MySpace Web sites that your teenagers want to visit.

Here's some bad news: Just as we learned from the great physicist Richard Feynmann, when he discovered that scientists working on the Manhattan Project could not manage their safes properly, so it is with the system administrations of many important computer systems. Whether it is a computer operator in a government or business setting, or a part-time system operator trying to keep the computers in the office running, the system administrative task is not generally performed in a consistent or reliable manner.

The problem, in a nutshell, is that computer system administration is too complicated. Take an afternoon to browse the relevant books on the topic in your local bookstore. Many of these system administrative guides are as voluminous as automobile repair manuals. Furthermore, the burden of our present computing model places almost all of the work for administering PCs on the end user.

"The tragedy of modern computing," writes Marcus Ranum, the security guru who installed the first Internet security protections into the White House computer systems, "is that we've turned nearly every man, woman, and child in the plugged-in world into a Windows sysadmin."

Computers require set-up and configuration activities that are beyond what is required for comparable appliances such as VCRs, televisions, and even automobiles. When you unpack your new computer and plug it into the Internet, you will soon find yourself installing software, dealing with unexpected crashes ("Daddy says to just turn the thing off and then back on again!"), and scratching your head about the inevitable Spam and viruses. But it wasn't always like this.

Two decades ago, users accessed computers with devices called dumb terminals. These devices, such as the popular VT100, consisted of no more than a keyboard and a screen with lousy graphics. We referred to these terminals as dumb because they were not general purpose processing machines.

But before you associate dumb with bad, consider that these terminals had some significant advantages. If you were having any sort of problem whatsoever with your terminal, then you simply walked over to the equipment closet, grabbed a new one, and plugged it in. There were no patches, viruses, software updates, or vulnerabilities. They worked pretty much all the time.

The mainframe, you may remember, could only be inspected physically through a glass partition, behind which the computer operators would tend to the machinery. Normal users weren't allowed anywhere near the actual computer. Even if you wanted something as simple as a copy of your printout, you stood in line by a little window outside the computer room. Someone would eventually emerge with your paper and glare at you for interrupting the important task of computer system administration.

Admittedly, this wasn't a convenient situation – we all hated waiting on those lines for print-outs. But the set-up had obvious security advantages. Organizations could centralize their complex system administration functions; they could put their best people on the task; and they could more easily enforce policies because administrative tasks only had to be done in one place. Security was easier, and most computer system environments were significantly more secure than the typical systems we find today.

(By the way, security was *easier* in those days, but not perfect. There were problems galore in early computer systems, especially in areas we take for granted today. Early users of shared operating systems might have found, for example, remnants of someone else's editing session on their screen. There were also reams of conditions that would cause nuisance and crashes, but these were not really security issues.)

In an early Bell Labs memorandum (one that seems to have disappeared from my files), I can recall researcher Rob Pike referring to powerful personal computers as "obnoxious office mates." I'd add that they provide a security burden on users that was totally unheard of in previous eras. As an example, most security chiefs today know that a single improperly administered personal computer can place an entire enterprise at risk. This places great responsibility on every employee to be extra careful.

Recall the example cited earlier about the domain controllers that were running in a seriously overloaded state. As was mentioned, the security team did the analysis and discovered that a tiny number of computers on the network were infected with a new variant of a virus. These systems, just a handful in total, were sending bogus requests to the domain controllers, thus degrading enterprise network performance. We were all amazed that *so few* infected computers could have such an effect.

To address the problems of bad system administration and their effect on security, I have some suggestions:

Secure Defaults: Vendors of software systems, especially operating systems, must deliver their products in a default secure configuration. We all know that many users, even those managing critical systems, often configure systems with little customization. Such an approach relies on manufacturer-set defaults for protection. As such, manufacturers should feel obliged to ensure that poor administrative choices do not place us all at risk. Software that filters email attachments, for example, should disallow *all* attachments by default, and only allow ones specifically designated for acceptance.[34]

Services Off By Default: When you buy a computer system, optional services should be turned off by default. *Period.* Anyone administering such a system would have the option of enabling only the services that are required locally. Software providers should perhaps view this as a potential marketing differentiator. They could possibly even charge more money for the default-secure configuration option. Most of the security managers I know would certainly sign up for such an option.

Centralized Administration: One step that would assist normal users considerably involves the centralization of certain system administrative services through remote, network-based management, perhaps in the wide area network. If this is done properly, one arrives at a model that should be comfortable to most users. Access and usage would be controlled by end-users, with all administrative tasks performed in a centralized, ubiquitous network environment. Some people have referred to this in the past as a thin client model. Network providers refer to this as a "clean pipe" solution.

System Administration as a Profession: Finally, in business and government settings, system administration must be viewed, especially for critical systems, as a legitimate profession. It is one that requires specialized skills, education, and training. The classic case of taking the most junior member of a team and adding system

---

[34]To my knowledge, no anti-virus vendor supports this obvious security method.

administration to the thousand other assigned daily tasks, is simply no longer acceptable. System administrators need to be treated, trained, and paid, as specialized professionals. Only then will we see the task performed in a more secure manner.

Lack of Diversity

There is an excellent chance that you have at least one computer in your home or office that runs a Windows-type operating system with the usual word processing, email, and spreadsheet applications. This computer is probably connected to the Internet through dial-up or broadband with a local Internet Service Provider, or through some virtual private network (VPN) that your employer sets up for you.

If a bad person successfully creates a virus program that attacks Internet-connected platforms running the software mentioned above, then the virus stands a good chance of getting to you. Sure, you might be hiding behind a firewall, but a good virus finds its way around such details, perhaps hiding in an email attachment or a Web command. Even your anti-virus software only works if the security company gets you a fix before the virus gets *you*.

If, on the other hand, you were using something different like a Unix machine on a non-Intel platform, then the likelihood of a typical sort of virus hitting you is considerably reduced. Sure, a virus might be coded for the Unix platform, but experience suggests that most viruses are not. Everyone knows that malicious code will be targeted where the greatest gain to the intruder can be found. If everyone runs the same code, then the attacks will target that code.

As such, *diversity* becomes an unexpected, but excellent preventive measure for the viruses, worms, and other Trojan horses that target our computer and network systems. Security expert Gene Spafford from Purdue has this to say about diversity in the context of software: "The dominant software architecture that runs our national defenses, underlies our public utilities, powers our government agencies, and supports our banks, medical establishments, and educational organizations is from one company."

The following two statements should be seriously considered in the context of increasing the resilience of cyber infrastructure from attack – especially if it involves critical national systems:

- *The Downside of Similarity*: Cyber attacks work better when the target computers and networks run the same software, operate on the same networks, utilize the same security protections, employ the same policies, and are functionally interoperable.

- *The Upside of Difference*: Cyber attacks work less well when the target computers and networks run different software, operate on separate networks, utilize different security protections, employ different policies, and are non-interoperable.

Mind you, interoperability is not an inappropriate requirement for computer systems. But the fact remains that if multiple systems look exactly the same across an infrastructure, then virus and worm programs will progress through that infrastructure more readily. Diversity counters this threat directly.

Many of my professional colleagues claim to have *never* thought about diversity in the context of computers, networks, and software. We're all so inundated with the usual story on interoperability, interconnection, and sameness in our computing environments, that thoughts of diversity are equated with immature and irresponsible waste. The very suggestion that computing decisions be made with diversity in mind is often viewed as reckless.

This observation strikes me as odd, given how most people see the benefits of diversity in different contexts. For example, we are taught in high school that when too much similarity exists in the plants, animals, and other organisms of an ecosystem, singular diseases can wipe out portions of that environment. "The opposite of biodiversity is referred to as monoculture," explains Kathy Paris from Access Excellence at the National Health Museum. "Because all of the species are identical, diseases can spread quickly."

We also know that people of diverse backgrounds and interests strengthen a society. Hence, social diversity makes for a more robust nation. Similarly, in business, we've learned over the years that industrial functions such as supply chain management work best in the context of diversity programs across multiple suppliers. The risks of problems developing with a single supplier are thus avoided.

The cyber infrastructure equivalent here involves sameness amongst software, computer, and network elements. On the Internet, for example, domain name system consists of one common service across the entire Internet. So if bad people take out this single infrastructure element (perhaps through denial of service), then the whole Internet could possibly stop working properly. There is no diversity here, just a single infrastructure.

As you might expect, having single points of attack in a critical infrastructure component is a no-no. It allows for single strategies to have broad reaching effects. "Centralized solutions are inherently risky," explains Peter Neumann from SRI International. "If everything depends on it, the design is a bad one."

Complex Network Architectures

Twenty years ago, network engineers had trouble connecting two different computers. Companies and government agencies would launch big projects to achieve connectivity between machines. These efforts often began with the design or selection of a suitable data network protocol, because no clear standard existed at the time. Computer communications was simply not an easy task in those days.

One of my first tasks at Bell Labs in 1985 involved establishing a secure communication link between several different computer systems in our laboratory. We were bidding on a project for NORAD, and we had created a special demonstration data protocol that worked reasonably well after a fashion. I still have a color snapshot in my desk of the lab configuration. It was little more than a bunch of small computers connected together via our protocol, but we were very proud that everything was working.

This situation is so laughable today, because with the advent of Internet technology and the Internet protocol, the process of establishing network connectivity between machines is trivial. In fact, I find myself repeating the following observation frequently to audiences around the world:

> *Twenty years ago, we didn't know how to connect computers. Today, we don't know how to separate them.*

Perhaps a more profound observation is that connectivity between computers has become so extensive that one can be reasonably confident that users of any computer system can find their way via some network path to virtually any other computer system. Sure, there may be firewalls located along the way, but for most intelligent hackers, these are little more than minor speed bumps. Here is this observation stated more succinctly:

> *Virtually every computer can be reached over a network from any other computer.*

Most organizations have so many network connections into and out of their enterprise that the best they can do to protect themselves is to herd all the connections together into traffic gateways. These gateways are obvious places to insert security devices like firewalls. But, as you'd expect, hackers and others have figured out clever ways to either go right through or around these firewall protected gateways.

For example, most firewalls allow Web traffic inbound and outbound. Attacks that ride over Web services, and many do, are thus quite difficult to stop with a normal firewall. The result of all this is a significantly heightened likelihood that your computer and mine can communicate over some network, probably traversing several organizational gateways, political and national boundaries, and intermediate systems in the process.

As an aside: I still find it amazing that keystrokes on my computer in New Jersey can fire up a Web process instantaneously on some faraway computer in Japan. There was a time when this sort of long distance connection was a very big deal. Remember when we all waited until after eleven PM to make long distance calls? Today, our children would consider this a ridiculous nuisance.

Back to our discussion: When cyber terrorists or criminals plan an attack on some target infrastructure, remote access to the target's assets is always a key component of the plan. Certainly any sort of cyber attack is greatly simplified if disgruntled insiders provide some assistance. And attacks can always be complemented by forced or surreptitious physical entry into a target premise. But it is much more likely that a cyber attack will be performed through entirely remote means without the need for insider support – a choice that is optimal from the perspective of cost, risk, and effectiveness.

A consulting team at AT&T performed a security analysis for a government agency several years ago. During the analysis, the team examined the various maps of connectivity that had been built by their engineers using automated tools and inventory management systems. You would not believe the rat's nest this exercise produced – and this was only for a small portion of the agency's overall network. Amazingly, as the team unraveled further the rat's nest into something that could be understood, a completely unprotected portion of their network was uncovered – one with direct connections to the Internet!

This experience illustrates the problems that emerges with unbridled complexity in a network infrastructure environment. Malicious remote access is perhaps the most serious of these problems. Such access could stem from employees leaving unnoticed connections to their office computers, engineers creating tough-to-find gateways to the Internet, and administrators having a poor understanding of the traffic being allowed into and out of a network.

Two decades ago, the great computer scientist, Tony Hoare, provided a sound warning about system complexity in his acceptance lecture for the prestigious Turing Award – the highest award given each year to a computer scientist. He explained in his lecture that if a computer system is too complicated for any one human being to completely understand in its entirety, then it is too complex. While he wasn't referring specifically to security, he certainly could have been.

As if things were not bad enough, the recent explosion of wireless networking will accelerate the complexity. The potential for anyone, including malicious intruders, to now scan the local airwaves for connectivity into all sorts of networks is frightening. Sure, there are means for using encryption and access control to deal with this threat. But many network owners – in fact, it seems safe to say *most* – simply don't bother.

The bottom line with respect to this vulnerability is clear: Massive connectivity of computers around the globe increases the risk of security attack. Certainly there are strategies that address the problem to a degree. Firewalls and intrusion detection systems can try to throttle and analyze traffic into and out of an enterprise; encryption can be used to protect data as it passes from one place to another; and software improvements must occur to reduce the number of vulnerabilities resident in end-points.

But none of these protections are even close to perfect – and purveyors of critical national cyber infrastructure must beware. The default global decision to simply connect everything to everything else has its security consequences.

Open Access to Organizational Data

Some time ago, I was sitting with the Chief Information Officer of a major corporation in California. She was explaining to me that her company had been experiencing security problems, as evidenced by odd changes found in their server configurations.

"We found strange and unknown dummy accounts that had been set up," she explained. "And we saw that certain system files had been altered in key servers. It was quite shocking!"

When I asked what her forensic team was finding, she explained that they were working off the theory that someone from the outside broke into the corporate network. In fact, this is why she was discussing the incident with me. Since AT&T was her Internet service provider, she wanted help from my team in improving the security of her network perimeter.

That's when I made my mistake:

"Could it perhaps have been one of your own people?" I asked innocently.

Her face immediately turned red and she looked at me crossly.

"Are you implying that this might have been caused by one of our employees?"

Uh, oh, I thought.

"Well … uh, yes," I said.

"Look, we trust our staff," she replied. "We view them as part of our family. They've never given me any reason to believe they would be dishonest. So my operating assumption is that someone must have broken in from the outside."

As you would expect, I dropped the subject – and we helped her improve the security of her perimeter. But the point of the story should be obvious: It is not easy for managers to accept that the people around them might be malicious. We all know what it's like to be around someone who is disgruntled, but the notion that such a person would intentionally sabotage a system is not easy to deal with.

Perhaps even more tough is for managers to consider accepting that their associates might be trying to gather information for the purposes of cyber terrorism. Information gathering by terrorist insiders represents a growing security threat that most managers have never bothered to consider. This is a shame, because it results in free reign to anyone who signs an employment contract.

As the world became obsessed with the World Wide Web a decade ago, a culture of information sharing emerged that was unprecedented in computing. Sensitive information that had previously been controlled suddenly morphed into content designed to lure visitors to Web sites. It didn't help that Wall Street was no longer valuing companies on the basis of financial results, but rather on *hits* to the company Web site. This spirit of information sharing, so fundamental to the adoption of the Web, certainly had its benefits, but security was not one of them.

Most organizational Intranets, for example, allow employees to access to a vast store of information through their browser. In almost every case I've seen, employees can visit internal sites to read company policies, learn about sales and marketing information, examine financial results, and even gain access to production or manufacturing control systems. It's pretty much an open door once you're on the inside.

If you consider that employees are increasingly transient into and out of companies, then what's to stop them from using their stay in a company to download proprietary data and intellectual property? Anyone can apply for a job at your company, work for a few days gathering as much information as they can store, and then move on to another company to do the same thing.

In contrast, military and intelligence organizations handle information in a more compartmentalized manner. This is good news, and as a result, these critical sectors are reasonably immune from inappropriate insider access. But other sectors of government in most nations, and almost all commercial organizations do very little to protect their information from insider access.

One development worth mentioning in this area is the emphasis that Sarbanes-Oxley has brought in the United States to improving controls in financial systems. One area of control involves so-called segregation of duty policies. While the requirement is generally expressed in a vague manner, focusing more on *write* access than *read* access, and while it only applies to systems related to financial book close, the regulation has significantly raised awareness in American public companies to the dangers of unregulated access.

Perhaps in the years to come, more emphasis will be placed on protecting information across a larger set of global organizations. But because current approaches are becoming so ingrained, and because of the huge cost efficiencies that on-line information provides, it is much more likely that this vulnerability will remain for a long time.

In the meantime, if you are a corporate information security officer, then I'd suggest you quickly take inventory of what can be found by insiders with browsers – and then take steps to minimize access to anything that would seem particularly sensitive.

Weak or Non-Existent Authentication

Suppose we just met for the first time and I wanted to identify myself to you. I'd state my name and extend my hand in friendship. We'd then clasp hands, you'd look me over, and that would be that. People follow this protocol every day. We don't refer to this process explicitly as authentication, but that's what it is.

Let's now suppose that I want to lie to you about my identity. I'd simply state a false name, we'd clasp hands, and unless you happened to have some other information, you'd know me by some false name. This is an example of weak authentication, because you have done very little (actually nothing) to validate what I am saying.

An obvious question is how this authentication process could be strengthened. One method would be for you to request a business card. If I produce a printed card with my name on it, you'd be inclined to accept my identity. But, of course, this card would prove nothing. Anyone can get a business card printed with any name on it.

Another approach would involve my providing a less forgeable document like a passport or driver's license. Producing such a document would go a long way toward validating identity because it's associated with an *issuing authority*. Nevertheless, even this process can be tampered with. I'm told, for example, that places exist in Manhattan where you can get a decent looking driver's licenses for cash. (I wouldn't know for sure.)

The authentication of identities on the Internet follows a roughly analogous pattern. A series of procedures of increasing strength can be used to identify one computer user or server to another. Passwords, for example, provide a common, but extremely weak form of authentication. Technologies such as smart cards and token identifiers provide a much stronger validation, one that cannot be easily spoofed. Even in computing, we have biometric identification that is pretty good, but not perfect.

With all of these options, you'd assume that the management of identities using authentication methods would be a slam-dunk, and you'd assume that establishing *anonymity* on the Internet would be pretty tough. Unfortunately, gaining anonymous access to the Internet for the purpose of initiating attacks is simpler than you'd expect – and the conditions for allowing such anonymity are not going to go away soon.

Recall that your broadband-connected home computer is not terribly anonymous. Your service provider knows your identity and assigns you an Internet protocol address. If necessary, the service provider can easily turn you over to the authorities. Granted, it might not be easy to determine whether Mom or the family seventeen-year-old is doing the hacking (or whatever), but the computer can be easily identified. Most cyber attacks are therefore not launched by the attacker's service account.

Computers sitting on corporate networks are also easily identifiable, but more by the internal network staff than any external authority. Furthermore, since most companies police their gateways, it is hard to imagine heavy cyber crime being initiated from someone's computer at work – except for the obvious case in which insider sabotage is occurring.

Stolen accounts are a popular way to hide one's self on the Internet. Normal citizens with dial-up accounts, or company employees with remote access accounts can easily have their access nabbed. This can occur by password guessing, or by infiltrating the management systems at the service provider. Both techniques are common, as evidenced by the plethora of stolen accounts that are for sale every day on underground hacker sites. (I would prefer to not offer references on this one.)

Once the bad guys have some stolen accounts, they can attack over the Internet with almost total impunity. And, to be honest, if your dial-up account is hacked and you are defrauded, it is unlikely that you will be held to blame for this. This reduces the urgency with which most people view this problem. As such, Internet attack using stolen accounts is a hugely popular approach – one that we should not expect to diminish in the coming years.

Malicious individuals also know that a so-called shell account on some Internet-connected Unix system provides a convenient starting point from which to attack systems. The idea here is that the attacker would use this system to launch attacks, especially if the system is not well policed. A typical such environment would be some computer sitting on an academic network, perhaps in a university, that is run by students and connected without security to the Internet. It does not help that most schools are firm about not restricting access to the Internet or even monitoring usage.

So the bottom line is that weak or non-existent authentication for Internet-based activity will continue as long as stolen accounts and shell accounts on unprotected systems abound. Since neither is likely to diminish soon, we will simply have to learn to live with the situation and do everything we can to reduce the associated risk.

Unprotected Broadband Communications

If you connect to the Internet using a modem and phone connection, your computer is assigned a temporary Internet protocol address. This address comes from a pool of available addresses that your service provider owns. As long as you are connected, your data goes out stamped with this address, and data comes back to you at this address.

When you hang up, you are no longer connected to the Internet, and you lose the address. This has the trivially obvious effect of protecting your computer from cyber attack – as long as it is turned off and not connected to any network. The result is that your information and identity are safe – for the time being. In addition, however, your system is no longer available for use in attacks aimed at other machines. This is an especially important consideration for computers that are not regularly updated with security software.

If, on the other hand, you connect to the Internet over a broadband service – and this includes WiFi, then a so-called *persistent* connection is established between your computer and the Internet. The persistent connection is maintained over your cable or digital subscriber loop (DSL) interface. Broadband connections thus allow you to keep your computer perpetually connected to the Internet. Sometimes broadband connections are referred to as *always-on* connections.

From the perspective of cyber security, your always-on connection is now an accessible component of the Internet. From the perspective of a cyber attacker, your system could be and is often used as a beachhead from which to launch subsequent attacks. The bad news is that proper system administration is the first line of defense for your computer – and we've already established that home users do not typically perform such administration properly.

A market has now sprung up with products that perform various types of security protections for home computers. These products include firewalls, intrusion detection systems, Spam removal systems, and virus filtering. The problem, unfortunately, is that very few people really know how to use these products properly – and when they do, the result is often inadequate. My children complain, for example, that the personal firewall installed on their computer changes the behavior of certain computer games.

Even more insidious is that every day, some unsolicited request arrives across most broadband connections demanding that the user renew a license for some critical security software that is expiring. This often leads to end-users renewing licenses for software that they do not even run on their systems. ("Let's see, hmmm, uh, did I buy Spam Grabber or Spam Killer?")

Another problem is that the cyber security software designed for home computers is just plain hard to understand. I have open in front of me now a user's guide for the security software I have installed on my family's home PC. As a test, I just closed my eyes and pointed my finger at random to an arbitrary sentence in the guide. Here's what I hit:

> *If you experience problems with installation or compatibility of DirectX on your computer, please consult the hardware manufacturers of your video or sound card for the latest drivers compatible with DirectX.*

I'm willing to admit – at the risk of receiving a thousand explanatory emails – that I have no clue what in the devil this means or whether it pertains to me. Furthermore, the likelihood that I would actually contact the manufacturer of my video or sound card is about the same as the likelihood that I would contact the manufacturer of the buttons on my television.

As a result, computers on broadband connections are, for the most part, poorly protected. Many Internet attacks are thus designed to take full advantage of this vulnerability. As we've suggested repeatedly, they exploit improper system administration and software vulnerabilities in these always-on systems as launching points for an attack. Maybe the attacker finds several thousand broadband connected launching points through scanning. By implanting code that harnesses these home machines, an attack can be initiated that will look like it's coming from thousands of unwitting broadband users.

This problem is rather serious, and very few good solutions are currently available. One thing I do know, however, is that the only solutions that will work must involve centralizing the protection of these machines. If we rely on home users to learn to perform proper security system administration, then this vulnerability will never go away. The best solution, perhaps, resides with uniform security solutions from broadband or Internet service providers. Time will tell whether these solutions become available and are successful.

Societal Dependence on Computing

We introduced earlier in this book the notion of an equation that measures security risk based on the likelihood and potential consequences of attack. Let's illustrate this risk concept in non-computing terms:

Suppose a criminal picks the locks outside your house, breaks in, and steals a pile of your things. Aside from being outraged, you now perceive your risk as increasing, simply because the likelihood of an attack seems so real (because it truly happened). Alternatively, if you put some items of greater value in your home, you also view the risk as increasing, simply because there is more now to lose.

It is this second component of risk – namely, the consequences of attack, that has had a profound increase on the risk of cyber security attack in most environments. In particular, our global dependence on computers and networks has resulted in an obvious increase in the risk that a successful cyber attack might occur – even if the likelihood of attack remains the same.

One aspect of this increased risk corresponds to something known as a non-specific attack. A cyber terrorist has two options in creating an attack. The first option involves a specifically targeted attack aimed at some system or infrastructure component. This might require reconnaissance or special knowledge for it to produce real value to the attacker.

The second option involves an attack that is non-specific. It could, for example, be broadcast over a network to hit anything in its path. This sort of attack requires little reconnaissance in advance, and is less likely to cause harm to some specifically designated target.

Internet worms are good examples of this second option, because they generally affect large numbers of unrelated systems on the Internet (except for the similarity in vulnerability being exploited). Such non-specific attacks raise security risk for everyone, especially those who believe that they are not targets.

Frequently, in my work at AT&T, I run into customers who claim that no security problem exists because their organization could not possibly represent a target.

"We are a clothing manufacturer," I might hear. "Why would anyone care to attack us?"

The answer is simple: If your network is reachable, then you are a target for a non-specific attack – regardless of whether anyone really cares about what you do.

Poor Cyber Security Awareness in Decision-Makers

Citizens of most countries view cyber security as a curiosity – one that simply does not rank as serious as more tangible forms of terrorism such as hijacking, bombings, and the unthinkable use of nuclear, biological, and chemical weapons.

 Expecting to change this perception through national awareness programs will have dubious results (remember our seatbelt and smoking analogies). But such naïve perception of the cyber security threat is especially troublesome when it occurs in national decision makers. It's sort of like medical doctors being unaware of the risk of smoking or bad eating.

In computing, such naïve understanding of the global cyber security risk creates an environment for most nations in which infrastructure security decisions are made based on bad information. Managers build information systems or Web sites in total ignorance of their security implications. As a result, security awareness and training programs are required in a focused high level manner so that senior decision makers have an accurate view of the threat.

Benjamin Netanyahu writes in his classic book *Fighting Terrorism* of a famous motto – *Obsta principiis*. The motto translates roughly as "oppose bad things when they are small." This motto seems well suited to the cyber terrorist threat we currently face. If we wait for cyber terrorism to become a much larger threat to the globe, then we will pay the consequences. It is better to take steps against this while it is still relatively small.

So what must be done? I believe each nation must immediately raise the awareness among our *infrastructure decision makers* of the challenges and risks associated with cyber terrorism. These decision makes include politicians, business leaders, academics, and any other individual or group with broad influence. The society of each nation must demand of its leaders more focused and effective protections against the terrible consequences that will occur when cyber terrorists decide to attack critical infrastructure.

6 Cyber Security Safeguards

T HE MAJOR THEMES IN THIS BOOK – correct software, improved system administration, and reduced system complexity – serve as a backdrop for the protection of cyber systems in virtually any context. That is, they *always* make sense, whether some individual or organization is explicitly addressing security properly or not.

In addition, however, specific security safeguards do exist for countering the risk of cyber attack. Some of these safeguards, such as the use of firewalls or intrusion detection systems, will be familiar to readers. Other approaches, such as the use of deception, might be less familiar.

A brief preview list of the security measures addressed in this chapter is offered below:

- *Access Control* – Authorization enforcement for assets
- *Audits* – Independent third-party assessments of security
- *Authentication* – Validation of reported identities
- *Biometrics* – Use of human attributes to authenticate
- *Cryptography* – Special codes to protect information
- *Deception* – Using false measures to trap bad guys
- *Denial of Service Filters* – Absorbing volume attacks
- *Ethical Hacking* – Good guy hacking to test security

- *Firewalls* – Guards that implement your policy for data traffic
- *Intrusion Detection* – Pattern-based surveillance for attacks
- *Response* – Actions taken after an attack is initiated
- *Scanning* – Test activity designed to detect weaknesses
- *Security Policy* – Rules defined by an organization for security
- *Threat Management* – Analysis of log files and security alarms

Our list of safeguards is by no means complete. But it does include most of the major security strategies that professional security experts use to reduce the risk of cyber attack.

Preliminary Comments on Safeguards

Here's something to keep in mind: Unless you are a professional in the security or computing industry, many of the key cyber security decisions about your system will be made by someone *other than you*. This is true for readers who use their PCs for day-to-day use, as well as for readers who are employees of companies with dedicated cyber security teams.

Certainly, users with PCs can decide which anti-spyware software to buy, and Internet users can reduce the risk of viruses by being careful about which sites they browse on the Web. Users can also try to select good passwords and exercise care in not writing these passwords down.

But the fact remains that the majority of core security safeguards are controlled and determined by four groups:

- *System and Software Developers*: This is where the effectiveness of a given security control is determined. Your anti-virus software, for example, is only as good as the technical decisions made by its developer.
- *System and Security Administrators*: This is where decisions on how software, applications, and services are set-up and controlled. In your company, this is probably a function of the

IT department. On your PC, the operating system vendor set things up in a manner that you'll probably not change dramatically.

- *Service Providers:* This is where decisions are made about which traffic should be allowed to proceed in which direction. Obviously, this is dictated by contracts with customers, as well as local laws.

- *Government:* This is where broad policy decisions are made that can affect security safeguards. Trade-offs between citizen privacy and safeguard effectiveness must be made here as well.

The fact that others control cyber security in most contexts should not reduce your enthusiasm in learning about how security safeguards work. Rather, you should feel empowered to influence decisions made by the four groups listed above. Government policy on cyber security, for example, is only weakly debated in most countries, and the discussion is generally dominated by experts. Now, you can join in.

Access Control

Access controls are motivated by the need to manage *which* users can do *which* operations to *which* data. They are based on the notion of an authorization policy for users. Access controls are mostly embedded in the hidden plumbing of the software we all use in our homes and businesses. So for the vast majority of readers, access control decisions are made by a separate corporate security team, or by the vendor of the software running on your PC.

Access control schemes follow an early conceptual tool for computer security known as the *reference model.* Established four decades ago by security pioneer, James Anderson, the reference model boils down all of computer security to a continuing stream of user requests that are either granted or denied.

"You want access to the corporate directory? Sorry, not allowed."

"You want to go through the corporate firewall? OK, fine."

"You want to get onto our Web site? Sure, go right ahead."

"You want to open records on the database? Sorry, no way."

In most cases (but not all), access controls consist of mechanisms placed into your system by a software developer, rather than something you would go out and purchase on your own. They do, however, provide users and administrators certain options on settings, but this varies considerably from one system environment to another. These settings can also be confusing.

Access controls on computer systems generally provide protections at two different levels:

- *Application Level:* If someone sends you a Word or Excel file that is password-protected, this is an example of an application level access control (albeit a weak one). Similarly, when a Web site demands a password before you can browse certain links, this is also an application level control. The idea is that controls are placed on *who* can do *what* to some software application.

- *System Level:* In contrast, if your computer is set to only allow administrative functions by the system owner, this is an example of a system level control. Usually, this level of control involves functions that are part of the underlying operating system (e.g., Unix, Windows). System level access controls correspond to the functions that reside closer to the hardware assets of a system.

Considerable attention has been placed on business access controls as part of Sarbanes-Oxley initiatives in the United States. One such control is that employee *duties* for relevant applications and systems must be partitioned and segregated. In other words, Sarbanes-Oxley requires that access controls be in place to ensure that no one individual can have too much power. So if you are the person who approves refund checks, then you should not also be the person who can send out the refund checks.

As a result of this attention, system administrators in many businesses are likely to do a better job controlling access to financial systems.[35] A common experience many administrators are reporting involves financial applications with so-called orphaned accounts. These are the accounts that have been sitting on a system, unused and dormant, probably because the employee the account belonged to left the company years earlier! Sarbanes-Oxley initiatives are forcing administrators to clean these accounts up and improve the general access control health of the environment. One group recently reported to me that tens of thousands of application accounts were deleted from their company systems, and not a single employee complained.

Perhaps more good news is that just as cleaning one room makes the others look messy, non-financial systems are now likely to be subjected to more rigorous controls as well. Controllers and information technology managers are already beginning to notice this obligation. The result is that so-called *identity management* systems are becoming more popular as a means for centralizing access controls for a large number of applications and systems. This is a positive trend.

Audit

Anyone in business who has ever been subjected to a security audit will describe the experience as being roughly equivalent to root canal.

Specifically, a security audit involves an independent assessment of the protection aspects of some system of interest by a third party organization. Many individuals and firms have grown rich providing this type of consultation service for corporations and government agencies. Some people like to refer to Sarbanes-Oxley, for example, as a full-employment act for auditors. I fully concur with this view.

---

[35] This claim is primarily focused on public companies in the United States, but the effect on the overall security community could be more broad.

The underlying foundational concept of security audit is two-fold: First, audits presume the existence of some well-defined set of security requirements. A security audit cannot be based on subjective notions of whether some system looks good or feels right. Rather, it really must be based on an explicit list of security requirements, usually expressed in both qualitative and quantitative terms.[36]

Second, audits presume that an organization cannot be trusted to do what it is supposed to do (after all, we're human, right?). They presume that someone independent must review the details of some system of interest, much as an investigator peruses a crime scene. This aspect of the auditing task requires at least a working level understanding of the systems being targeted, which can be tough in complex technical environments.

Here is an illustration: Some years ago, my team was subjected to an audit that involved numerous Unix-based systems. The auditors noticed that the access control permissions were different from what was specified in the requirements documents. As a result, the systems were given a failing grade, and a lot of nasty emails ensued. What the auditors misunderstood, however, was that the settings were different from the requirements because they were more *restrictive* than what was required. We'd failed the audit for being more secure.

One industry improvement that is long overdue in the audit community involves commonality among the various audit standards. It is unacceptable that organizations must submit to so many different and incompatible audit standards, especially when most security standards fundamentally require the same basic things. The typical organization might, for example, have to submit to the following types of security audits:

- Sarbanes-Oxley for publicly traded American firms,
- ISO/17799 for companies doing business in Europe;
- HIPPA for health care firms,

---

[36] Auditors do, however, perform audits without requirements. "Your system is missing *something*," the auditor might comment. "I'm just not sure what."

- SAS 70 for firms in the financial industry,
- PCI requirements for companies that process credit cards,
- and on and on and on.[37]

The typical organization of the future – one would hope – should need to submit to one global security requirements auditing standard, one that would meet the needs of multiple constituents at an appropriate level. Cyber systems should have something like an Underwriter's Laboratories (UL) sticker. I am unaware of any substantive initiatives currently being worked by auditors along these lines.

Authentication

The most basic unit of computer security involves authentication, also known as the validation of a reported identity.

Stated more simply, security decisions are generally made based on *who* is requesting access to some resource, like a network or a Web site. So naturally, the ability to prove identity emerges as a fundamental security issue. It's at the heart of all security policy implementations, and is thus critical to countering the risk of security attacks.

Amazingly, the majority of authentication methods in use today involve passwords over networks. If you use a local service provider to dial onto the Internet, for example, then you probably do so with a password. If you try to protect your PC from others, then you probably do so with a password-protected screen saver. If you send files that you don't want others to see, then you probably protect those files with some sort of password.

For those who use broadband access to the Internet, a special type of password is used, one that is based on the network address of

---

[37] Use Google to decode the acronyms if you must, but I wouldn't waste the time. Ten security experts in a room probably couldn't expand the letters in HIPPA.

the router located with the subscriber. Such address information is set by the provider and is invisible to the user. But in some cases, the address can be spoofed. Nevertheless, once a computer is connected through a broadband router, it is considered by the provider to be authorized for access.

There have been many reported cases of youngsters connecting their PCs to WiFi routers located in their neighborhood to gain unfiltered broadband access to the Internet. I've even heard of youngsters tricking an unwitting neighbor into setting up unfiltered Internet access. ("Hi, Mr. Jones, uh, my Mom wouldn't let me use this WiFi router, so, uh, would you like it for your house? Oh, and uh, could you put it in that room that's right across from my bedroom?")

Any type of password authentication lies at the *weakest* end in a spectrum of possible security choices. (Cryptographic authentication lies at the opposite end. More on this later.) This is not to say that using passwords is wrong for normal PC users. It merely suggests that one shouldn't expect great security results when passwords are employed on networks.

From the perspective of enterprise network management, however, passwords are unacceptable, especially for remote access. In fact, this is such a strong consideration, that it can be stated as a basic rule:

Authenticating remote access to an enterprise network must involve something other than a password.

There are no exceptions to this rule. If someone in Pakistan can gain access to your corporate Intranet in London with nothing more than a password or series of passwords, then you basically have no security.

Two years ago, I visited with the security managers of a retail business. They explained that budget pressures forced the use of passwords. I suggested upgrading to hardware tokens, but they mostly yawned. Several months later, I saw in the news that they'd been hacked and that customer information had been compromised. I couldn't help but remember the yawns.

Biometrics

Everyone seems to be talking about biometrics as the magical answer to the world's security woes. While such claims are a bit of a stretch, the technology can be useful.

Biometric identifiers such as retinal patterns, voice tones, facial features, or fingerprints are more difficult to forge than passwords. This is not to say, of course, that biometric forgery is impossible. For instance, forged fingerprints on silicon jelly have been tricked readers into improperly identifying an individual. There have also been instances of facial recognition systems being tricked by a person simply holding up a picture.

But without question, such forgeries require considerable effort on the part of the intruder, much more than is involved in guessing or stealing a password. As such, many people have grown enthusiastic about biometrics. Officials in Tampa, Florida and Virginia Beach, for example, have installed biometric systems as part of enhanced security measures. Similar efforts using biometrics are on going around the world. (Perhaps you even encountered one today.)

Unfortunately, in spite of the promise associated with biometrics, security experts worry about the complex infrastructure required to support such an approach. One challenge in this infrastructure is that if your biometric pattern is compromised – and remember, computers store such patterns as strings of zeroes and ones – then you are in trouble, because you cannot change biometrics. If a hacker steals your retinal pattern, for instance, then you are out of luck, because your retina cannot be changed! (Tom Cruise movies to the contrary.)

Other problems exist as well. As people age, their features change. It can be as short as eighteen months before large percentages of facial recognition systems begin to fail in a target group. Also, a certain percentage of people will not have the required body part for biometric enrollment. Some estimates place this at a few percent of any reasonably sized group. It is also true that certain occupations such as masonry result in the destruction of fingerprints beyond all recognition.

Infrastructure solutions have certainly been proposed to deal with these challenges. For example, to deal with the aging issue, you could simply require users to re-enroll every year. If your population includes people with missing fingers, then set up multiple biometric enrollment systems and let people choose their method (which could come in handy in countries with laws that might protect those with disabilities.)

A decent rule of thumb for current technology is that biometric methods are likely to be most useful in smaller, well-defined environments such as campus networks or data center facilities. They are likely to be more prone to failure, primarily due to the crushing burden of providing scalable infrastructure, in places where the population is large and unconstrained. This obviously includes the Internet.

Cryptography

Several years ago, I was asked to spend a day in Washington D.C. discussing cyber security with one of the major political parties in the United States. This party (I won't tell you which) was run from two buildings in Washington connected by a so-called T1 line. This type of connection transmits roughly a million and a half bits every second.

In preparation for my visit, this group explained that they were concerned that their political opponents might tap into the T1 to steal secrets. "We could lose the next election to those political thieves," said my contact over the phone. So I came down to Washington to discuss encryption options for their T1 line.

When I arrived at their building, I noticed that the door was open, so I walked into their entrance room, and sat down at a small table. During the next hour, I sat there waiting, as absolutely *no one* came into or out of the office, except for one guy in a biking outfit ("Hey, dude," he said as he wheeled his bike into and then out of the office). Later, I signed for a UPS package.

After that hour, I got fidgety and started to wander around. Lo and behold, in my meanderings around this deserted office space, I happened to find in one of the offices – the office doors were open (ahem), and I just peeked inside – none other than a couple of computers and a low-end network router device.

Most security experts knew at the time that you could remove the need for passwords on that particular router by first powering it down. Then, when the device started coming back up, you typed control-B at the console, and after typing a simple command, you'd force the router to not ask for a password. The result of all this was that you now owned the router, and perhaps the entire network in that office.

So here's my question: Should this political party have been worrying about cryptography? Or should it have first attended to basic questions of infrastructure security, such as locking the doors? The use of cryptography in such a scenario would have been a tremendous waste of time. Unfortunately, this could be argued for most uses of cryptography in insecure environments.

The great Gene Spafford from Purdue has the best comment on this situation. He says that: "Cryptography on the Internet is like using an armored car to deliver money from a guy living on a park bench to a guy living in a cardboard box." He has it exactly right. If the computers and networks that surround your use of cryptography are insecure, then the effectiveness of the cryptography must be considered suspect at best.

As a security chief, I rely on encryption in computer, network, and service infrastructure every day, and I can think of a thousand places where you might rely on it as well. But in the end, cryptography only works if the environment is secure. And it only serves to provide security risk management in the following two ways:

- *Transit.* Cryptography is most useful for protecting data from malicious eavesdropping or tampering while it is in transit. This makes cryptography especially useful for authentication protocols, since they require short-lived, secret back-and-forth handshakes. Popular examples include IPSec, Secure Shell (SSH), and Secure Sockets Layer (SSL).

- *Storage.* Cryptography is somewhat useful for protecting data from disclosure or tampering at rest. Unfortunately, the key management problem for data in storage is greatly exacerbated by the fact that the data may be long-lived. As a result, encryption schemes for stored data are less common and less successful.

Another obvious consideration in the use of cryptography is its implications on the security of a given nation. That is, if criminals use cryptography to make their conversations secret, then law enforcement cannot easily eavesdrop. As a result, the US government has attempted, on various occasions, to limit the use of cryptography. Opponents claim this has the effect of actually make America less secure.

"The US government's restrictions on cryptography in the 1990's," writes Phil Zimmerman, author of a popular software encryption package called PGP, "have weakened US corporate defenses against foreign intelligence and organized crime." Only time will tell how this story plays out in the law enforcement community. My guess is that in ten years, law enforcement will come to rely on encryption for its operations more than any other group.

And in its place, a new form of security will emerge that will provide law enforcement with a much more effective means to catch bad guys in the act of talking too much: *Deception.*

Deception

Imagine the professional thief entering a posh jewelry store in the dead of night. The thief tiptoes toward the glass-enclosed case. Low voltage lights around the perimeter of the room cast an eerie glow across the room. Inside the glass case, the perfect diamond is perched up onto a soft, black felt base (it always seems to be black felt).

The thief rubs the tips of his gloved fingers together and then carefully opens the case and reaches – ever so slowly – toward the diamond. He holds his breath as his fingers inch closer to the prize. Just as he is about to grasp the jewel, there is a loud poof heard in the room. The lights go on. The glass case disappears.

Law enforcement officials are standing around him. He's been trapped. There is no jewelry store. It's a sting operation that was designed to lure him and catch him in the act. He curses himself at such stupidity to have been trapped this way. The law enforcement officials who put in him cuffs are smiling because they have a video recording of the entire episode. Conviction will be a piece of cake. *Sigh.*

You may think that this is a ridiculous scenario. But in cyber space, believe it or not, this sort of trap operation is becoming more and more feasible. In his book, *Honeypots: Tracking Hackers*, Lance Spitzner describes a computer attack spree by two hackers named J4ck and J1ll. "What J4ck and J1ll did not realize," writes Spitzner, "is that everything they had just accomplished was watched and captured by a group of security professionals because one of the computers they had hacked into was a honey pot."

Here's a definition: A honey pot involves creating a bogus, yet believable computer system that could entice terrorists to think that they've violated your space. It's amazingly similar to the jewelry store sting just described – only in some ways, it's *better.*

Let's look at a simple example: Suppose you're a bad person sitting in front of my computer and you are trying over and over to guess my password. Suppose further that someone has helped me rig the software on my computer with a deceptive honey pot. Perhaps the honey pot waits until the tenth bad guess and then simply allows you into a phony version of the system.

"It worked," you would mumble to yourself, "and it only took me ten guesses." Of course, because of the honey pot, you would not actually be allowed into the system on the tenth guess. The deception would have been established to trick you into thinking that you were successful. (Yes, I know that sometimes you might be innocent in your guessing.)

Thus, in our example, the honey pot doesn't really let you into my real computer. It instead creates a bogus view of the machine, maybe with fake files and icons. The juicy part of all this is that special security monitoring tools would be watching what you're doing. So, if you decide to look around for interesting files, the system would dutifully record this.

If you're wondering where you could buy such a thing for your home computer, then forget it. The very few honey pot tools that do exist have been designed for government, corporate, or research settings, and all have been designed for powerful servers. So if you walk into your local *CompUSA* and ask for honey pot software for your home computer, they will think you're nuts.

As you might guess, one important security requirement in all of this is for the honey pot environment to be realistic. If it looks like an obvious fake, then the attacker's suspicions will rise and the honey pot will not work. It would be like a thief glancing up at an obviously phony surveillance camera and waving facetiously as he steals merchandise.

The Honeynet Project is a research effort involving a loose consortium of security experts collaborating on the design and operation of a deceptive network. The project is described in the book, *Know Your Enemy*. One point made in the book is that realism must be carefully considered in the design of a honey pot: "You may want to create an environment within the Honeynet that replicates your organization," the researchers explain. "This will create a more realistic environment that, as Max Klinger, the team psychologist says, 'helps keep the Honeynet sweet.'"

In this sense, honey pots can be viewed as establishing sting operations. Cliff Stoll, the noted astronomer turned computer security expert, chronicled the use of an on-line sting operation in his wonderful book, *The Cuckoo's Egg*. "Give the guy what he's looking for," Stoll writes. "Create some files of phony information, laced with bogus secret documents."

The most common current applications of stings on the Internet today are centered on catching child molesters and similar types of criminals who use the Internet to stalk their prey. The FBI's Innocent Images program, for instance, involves active undercover investigations by agents in newsgroups and Internet Relay Chat (IRC) channels.

Tom Pickard, former assistant director of the FBI's Criminal Division, describes a case in which a man had been on the Internet surfing for young girls. "He was trying to have a young girl, or what he thought was a young girl, travel across state lines for the purposes of having sex with him," Pickard explains. "He followed up his suggestions with a bus ticket and agreed to meet this alleged young girl on the mall of the Smithsonian. He met two 200-pound FBI agents instead."

The U.S. Customs Service also actively utilizes deception for catching such criminals. They report that their Child Pornography Program has resulted in a three-fold increase in suspects being brought into custody since 1995. As you can see, American law enforcement understands deception and uses it effectively for certain types of crimes. They just don't use it enough today to catch cyber terrorists.

Surprisingly, other branches of American government – especially the Defense Department – have been somewhat ambivalent about the use of active deceptive techniques. Certainly, you will find the occasional row of inflatable tanks used as decoys in battle, but from what I've been able to find, Americans have used deception only sparingly in battle.

Jon Latimer, author of the fine book, *Deception in War*, claims that American commanders have often viewed deception as a survival technique to be used only in times of weakness. "In the West," he explains, "deception is often viewed as immoral, and more then one authority has claimed that, as a result, Americans resort to deception only reluctantly or else do it poorly."

This generally pejorative view of deception has found its way into American academia. Honey pots, in particular, are almost never studied. "Historically," writes Lance Spitzner, "honey pots have had a clouded reputation." To my knowledge, not a single academic institution in the U.S., or anywhere else, for that matter, is currently sponsoring an active and *prominent* research program in computing-based deception. On a personal note, I wrote a draft chapter on deception for a computer security text several years ago and one reviewer from a prominent university demanded that it was not appropriate for publication!

Take a glance at the published computing curricula from our finest American colleges and universities. You'll find absolutely no mention of deception in any of the course outlines. This is a terrible shame, because the possibilities for enhanced security through deception are endless. Perhaps our universities would be well advised to de-emphasize redundant programs in applied cryptography and to direct these energies toward advancing the art and science of deception in computing.

Now, I know that deception is just a fancy name for trickery. I also know that the technique, if improperly used, could cause normal, law-abiding citizens to get caught into stings by accident. I also know that intentionally luring a victim into a deceptive system is not a reasonable technique. So, yes – all of these concerns are reasonable and must be addressed.

But we should not use these issues as excuses to avoid examining and researching the proper use of deception. The situation we have currently involves the usual type of scorn one finds in a truly revolutionary new method – one that goes against the grain of the norm. The sooner we realize this, the sooner we can start to effectively use deception to improve commercial infrastructure, as well as national security.

And how, specifically, does all of this deception help protect infrastructure? It's simple: Deception by defenders produces uncertainty. Imagine yourself the evil cyber terrorist scanning United States critical infrastructure and finding barrels of different vulnerabilities. If you suspect, however, that the wily Americans have chosen to deploy deception, then you will question whether the vulnerabilities are real, or planted. This is a powerful, profound, and potent means for cyber defense.

Furthermore, this defense, more than any other, is well suited to address the central problem with system vulnerabilities. Recall the case made earlier that we cannot expect to remove all vulnerabilities from systems, especially software. With deception, we introduce the creative result in which by potentially adding new fake vulnerabilities, or at least the appearance of new vulnerabilities, we introduce uncertainty into a cyber terrorist group.

Denial of Service Filters

To understand how most enterprise-oriented denial of service tools work, consider the following simple image:

Imagine yourself standing on a beach with a yardstick in your hand. You wish to measure and monitor the rise and fall of the tide, so you drive the yardstick into the sand, and then as the rise of the tide reaches some point on the stick, you carefully mark this point with some duct tape. Then, you stand and watch as the tide goes down off the stick, and then up perfectly to your tape mark on the stick.

You have now done the equivalent of installing a denial of service detection tool at your enterprise gateway. The notion here is that if a tidal wave begins, you will see the water rise above the mark on your stick, and you will take rapid steps to deal with the problem. In a computing sense, these steps include trying to divert extra traffic, or throttling flows away from key resources.

Unfortunately, this approach does not work for any non-trivial event. Certainly, if a minor denial of service event hits the enterprise gradually, then such a method could be useful. But for the major sorts of denial of service events one finds on the Internet today, there is only one acceptable solution: Carrier-based filtering, far up-stream in the wide-area network.

In essence, such carrier-based filtering is like using a thousand yardsticks with tape marks, but placing these sticks five miles out in the ocean, where small perturbations are measured. When these minor disturbances begin to build up, filtering is done massively and in parallel, long before the many smaller problems can combine at the enterprise gateway into one huge problem.

My prediction is that in the coming years, two major events will occur to make the denial of service problem somewhat moot: First, tier one Internet carriers will continue to make investments in this technology, thus rendering the denial of service attack more trouble than it is worth. And second, DSL and cable providers will begin simple profile-based filtering of upstream activity from PCs. This will make the familiar distributed denial of service schema far less attractive.

Ethical Hacking

I have a small cartoon taped to the door outside my office in the Shannon Laboratory at AT&T Labs. It shows an awakened and startled couple lying together under the covers in their bed as an intruder stands at the foot of their bed. He is dressed obviously as a salesman and he is holding some sort of product in his hands and says, "May I interest you in a home security product."

This cartoon illustrates the view held by most experts on ethical hacking. On the one hand, it is patently ridiculous to have to demonstrate via hacking that a given enterprise is vulnerable. For virtually any organization with modern computer systems, applications, and networks in the most common configurations, I can assure you that such break-ins are quite possible.

By way of analogy, suppose that a home inspector is writing a report on the safety features of your home. If the inspector notices that a window is unlocked, does he really have to dive through into your basement to demonstrate that a break-in is possible?

I have learned, however, that some managers, especially more traditional ones for whom technology remains an unwelcome and unpleasant component of business, often need the two-by-four between the eyes of having someone demonstrate actually breaking into the enterprise. As such, this sort of activity – so long as it is carefully planned – should be considered acceptable.

One major caveat that I recommend to anyone considering an ethical hack is that detailed remediation and recovery plans be demanded beforehand. Far too many ethical hacks get somewhat out of hand, and real systems can be damaged.

One more thing: never, *ever* attempt a mock denial of service against your own system. There are no exceptions to this rule. Too many things can go wrong.

Firewalls

My first introduction to Internet firewalls came in 1993 when Steve Bellovin of AT&T sent me the pre-publication galleys for his historic book – written with Bill Cheswick – entitled *Firewalls and Internet Security*. The book absolutely floored me, not just because it was such a delight to read, but also because it implied a future that was almost impossible for me to imagine at the time. To be honest, I still can't believe how things have shaped up in the past decade. Let me explain:

Before the nineties, the vast majority of enterprise networking was done using private line connections provided by phone companies. That is, if your New York and San Francisco offices had to be connected, you called up your telecommunications carrier and asked for a private, circuit-switched link. The carrier would maintain secure operations to ensure that your link was actually private, and that was that. You didn't need or use a firewall. Things were relatively simple.

But then the Internet happened, and it truly changed everything. Suddenly, you had to worry about what would happen in New York if the guys in San Francisco were connecting to the Internet. You had to worry at Company X about the implications of connecting to Company Y. If they made bad decisions and allowed all sorts of hackers into their network, then you had to presume that these hackers could then get onto your network.

The security principle known as *transitive trust* is how Bellovin and Cheswick described the situation. Specifically, if Alice trusts Bob, and Bob trusts Eve, then Alice trusts Eve. This transitive property of network security led to things getting really ugly, because the conclusion everyone adopted was that you could no longer trust anyone. In short, you – and every other person and business on the globe – needed a firewall.

Thus, a new industry was born – one that delighted in selling you or your business a firewall (or several of them) to keep the bad guys out of your network. Military terms and analogies were used across this industry to increase sales. Your network became a fortress inside a perimeter, external business partners were viewed with distrust and suspicion, and the network on which the firewall was located became known as a demilitarized zone or DMZ.

My back-of-the-envelope estimate on the size of the firewall market goes thus: There are easily 100,000 organizations globally that spend about $100K annually on firewall-related salaries, license costs, and other miscellaneous costs. This guess is balanced by the fact that large banks spend much, much more than $100K annually on firewalls, whereas many small businesses probably spend less.

Anyway, doing the math, suggests an organizational annual spend of $10B, which is not chump change.

This brings me back to my first reading of Bellovin and Cheswick's book. What I find so astounding is that this basic notion of transitive trust introduced in their book represented the birth of a $10B industry. The incredible irony is that the carriers could have embedded this functionality into their networks in the mid-Nineties – but did not.

A further irony is that with the complexity of most modern networks, it has become so impossible to figure out the actual enterprise perimeter, that most organizations have been forced to order up many firewalls to plug all the leaks. The result is that firewall companies prey on the inefficiencies and poor architectural decisions of the modern organization. I've seen some companies with five hundred firewalls. I have no idea how they must manage them (or not).

The future of firewalls seems obvious to me: This functionality will become gradually embedded into the carrier infrastructure, which is where it originated from. Telnet packets destined for some enterprise will be either blocked or permitted, based on the reported policy of the receiving entity. Firewall audit logs will be combined together and used as the basis for a centralized correlation, hopefully resulting in faster incident response. Extensions of firewall processing such as intrusion detection will also find their way into the carrier infrastructure (see next section below).

Furthermore, the process of filtering viruses and Spam will become a passé feature in firewalls as more organizations rely on their carriers to provide so-called clean pipes into the enterprise. It is worth mentioning here that desktop anti-virus software will diminish in importance in the security industry in coming years. More likely, these commodity functions will become absorbed into the software we purchase and use from our operating system and application vendors. It would also be nice to hope that software correctness will improve to the point where viruses will be less prevalent as well.

So what are the implications on this $10B firewall industry? My guess is that in a few years, the firewall industry as a separate entity becomes a forgotten artifact of a post-Internet birth era that was willing to accept some costly inefficiency in order to maintain short-term order. The functionality and policy enforcement will migrate to the carrier.

Intrusion Detection Systems

An intrusion detection system, or IDS, is basically a surveillance camera for a network or system, albeit one that looks for security indicators rather than any sort of user content or data. And just like any type of surveillance, it comes with its distinct advantages and disadvantages. Let's start with the advantages:

First, an intrusion detection system generally operates in a passive manner. This means that it will not degrade your environment if it goes down or begins to go completely haywire. Most people are very comforted by this fact, because intrusion detection systems are known to go haywire from time to time.

Second, intrusion detection systems provide a real-time view into the bad sorts of things that could be happening. Generally, one inserts signatures and patterns of various sorts into an intrusion detection system, and then a pattern matching-type function progresses. So if you want to know when users are trying to repeatedly guess passwords, your intrusion detection system will help.

Now for the disadvantages: Like any surveillance method, intrusion detection only works if there *really is* someone seated behind some console trying to interpret what is being captured. This can become rather tedious, especially in large complex environments. Big companies and organizations have created 24/7 operations centers solely to house the staff watching the output from these systems. *Yawn.*

In addition, creating suitable signatures and patterns that correspond to attacks is quite difficult. In fact, this is so difficult, that many experts believe this invalidates the use of intrusion detection as a primary security system. Rather, one is wise to consider intrusion detection as a complement to existing security protections.

A somewhat telling anecdote that illustrates the problems associated with intrusion detection occurred recently on a network operated by a company I am aware of. They had several intrusion detection systems on their externally facing connections, mostly because they had needed to pass an audit. Over lunch, their CISO confessed to me that a week or so had passed during one span in which the intrusion detection systems had gone down.

And yes, you guessed it, no one noticed.

By the way, an intrusion prevention system, or IPS, is an intrusion detection system that is not passive. Rather, it tries to detect problems and then rectify them by inserting rules – usually called shuns – that block offending sources. I've always likened an intrusion prevent system to the situation in which one hands a gun to a blind man. Now this does not imply that intrusion prevention is not worth being considered. But the decision must be made in full recognition of the drawbacks that exist.

Response

When an electrical engineer designs a circuit that does not work, the proper resolution is to simply redesign the bad circuit. One would not expect some sort of "incident response" circuitry to be added to compensate for the bad design. This is just not the way an electrical engineer would handle it.

In contrast, if an information technology component such as a local area network or software system shows that it has systemic problems, the response is to create a real time process for handling the effects of such problems. Example processes include corporate incident response and software patch management.

Such emphasis on passive response rather than active removal is curious. I've often joked that it stems from the large number of astronomers in computing from academia (usually lured by paychecks). Astronomers like to recline on a hill and gaze up at the stars, knowing full well that they cannot change the observed configuration. I wonder if these same astronomers lean back in their swivels looking at the Internet, and view it as some naturally occurring phenomenon that also cannot be changed.

The bad news for most security professionals is that incident response will likely remain a fundamental component of any network and information technology program for many years to come. The stubborn security manager who decides that responding to problems is not good engineering, will likely be fired in the wake of catastrophe after catastrophe. One can and should have opinions, but one must also be realistic.

Regarding the optimal way to build an incident response team in a company, there appears to be two different models. The first model is the so-called "casual draft," in which people from all over an organization are coaxed (or pushed) into participating in response activities when something happens. Usually, such people already have fifty other jobs, so incident response becomes – and is sometimes referred to as – the fifty-first job. The disadvantages of such overloading are obvious.

A balancing advantage of this model, however, is that the best and brightest from an organization can be drafted. Furthermore, the people brought into the incident response function are often the closest to the actual infrastructure being affected. The experts at routing, desktop applications, and intrusion detection, for example, become de facto members of incident response.

The second model for incident response involves a dedicated team. In some organizations, this can be done with employees – albeit not without considerable expense. In other organizations, the function is outsourced to an external firm that specializes in such things. Both cases ensure that incident response professionals address the work as their primary work activity. But in both cases, the response work is still somewhat removed from the actual custodians of the infrastructure affected.

Scanning

Not tool long ago, security engineers from my team contacted me in a frenzy. I was told that during the course of a routine, and extremely light scan of our address space, nineteen servers had crashed. This was obviously not good, because I knew full well the internal headline that would follow: "Overly aggressive security team takes out servers with their hacking tools!"

In reality, what had happened was that a single "TCP open" in our scanners had somehow caused already corrupted network interface software to recycle. I was amazed that such a minor action could cause such problems, especially since I'd always made fun of the silly and popular delusion of some single packet of death that could take out a big network like the Internet.

I'm still not convinced that a single packet can take out the Internet, but I would strongly recommend that you use scanners with extreme care – even if they are doing nothing more than a ping or TCP handshake. My comments are amplified, obviously, if you are running active agents that perform deep inspection into the operating system or applications. These are powerful, but potentially dangerous tools, and they must only be used in the proper set of circumstances.

In particular, scanning systems and their agents should never be connected to poorly controlled infrastructure, such as easily accessible console functions. They should also run with the minimum possible privilege, which I fully recognize must often be root (gulp). Furthermore, remote scripting and other programming features should only be used if absolutely necessary.

The outlook for security scanning functions in an organization is mixed. On the one hand, it will remain critically important to have constant scanning to ensure that network ports are not improperly opened and that operating system and application configurations are consistent with policy. But in time, these rote commodity functions will be embedded into larger system management functions, and will thus seem to disappear.

The only groups that should care about such integration are those who sell scanning software. For the rest of us, this housekeeping chore should only get easier.

Security Policy

During one of the lectures in my graduate cyber security course at the Stevens Institute of Technology, I ask the students to design a suitable security policy for the firewall at the university. The purpose of the exercise is to help them recognize the arbitrary nature of most policy decisions.

For example, some student will invariably blurt out that URL screening for outbound Web browsing is not needed. I'll ask why, and most of the class will simply smile. Then someone will suggest that services like Telnet and FTP are important because sometimes people need them. And it generally goes on and on like this until we have something written down.

From a foundational perspective, the process we follow in the exercise is basically this: We figure out what everyone in the organization needs, and then set the rules to accommodate their requirements. In essence, this defines the first type of security policy that one sometimes finds. It can be referred to as the collective union policy, because it simply combines all requests into a policy.

There are obvious drawbacks to this sort of policy. If individuals or groups within the organization request services that are blatantly insecure, then they might place the larger organization at risk. Furthermore, requests could be made for services that are not legitimate. In fact, many normal users on a typical campus network don't really even know what they need.

The vast majority of instances for both large and small networks is done centrally by a security group. On the surface, such an approach would seem difficult to criticize as long as user requirements are taken into account. But organizational security policies often suffer from being overly complex, poorly written, and impossible to enforce.

One area of cyber security that deserves increased attention by managers in the coming years involves this notion of security policy enforcement. This will be tough, because when security improvements must be made that are considered inconvenient, it is the rare manager who will come down on the side of security. But the obligation here cannot be ignored; in fact:

> *Business managers make their most substantive contribution to increased cyber security by enforcing policy.*

Threat Management

Make believe you're back in college. A late night case of insomnia has you doing what most of my computer science students do under such circumstances: You're staring bleary-eyed into a glowing computer monitor, having a peek around the campus network.

In the course of your poking, you happen to find the computer server that I connect onto and use every day. And, by chance, you happen to notice a directory on this machine labeled with my name. Interesting, you think to yourself. I wonder what files he's got stored in this directory.

Intrigued, you tappety-tap here and clickety-click there. And before you can say the phrase 'breaking and entering,' you're gazing at a list of files belonging to your professor. And now for the fun part: You notice that one of the files is named 'midterm.' And it just so happens that we're having a midterm exam tomorrow. You look at the file details and realize that I created it today.

"Oh, my gosh," you mutter to yourself. "I've found the midterm."

So, what would you do? Would you look at the midterm? We both know that if you live by some reasonable code of ethics, then you would probably not look. But cyber terrorists are not deterred by ethical considerations – so forget that.

But now here's a new rub: Would you look at the file if you knew that a log of your activity was being recorded as you tappety-tap and clickety-click away? The logging function would be like some computer-based surveillance videotape of your activity.

"Log files can contain a large amount of information about an individual's use of a computer and can be an excellent source of digital evidence," writes Eoghan Casey in his book, *Digital Evidence and Computer Crime*.

So would the presence of logs influence whether you looked at the file? When I ask my graduate students at the Stevens Institute this question, roughly half say that they would be deterred from looking. You should know, however, that my best students, the ones often doing security administration for the university computer network, generally respond with a smile that no such logging function would ever deter them.

Here's what they mean: Let's examine logging in the context of those little surveillance cameras you sometimes see in retail stores. This will help us identify and explain the important issues without getting all caught up in computer-related detail.

Make believe you're a crook and you just walked into the local Hallmark store. You need a birthday card for your mother (even crooks have mothers) and you plan to steal one. While you're browsing up and down the aisles, you notice one of those little cameras. There it is, up in the corner of ceiling, and it's pointed at you.

So you walk over and have a peek. The camera seems to be real. It has a little light on the top and a cable poking back into a hole in the wall. Intrigued, you wander over to the cashier and find a wall of computer surveillance monitors rivaling the command center at

NORAD. Wow, you think. These people really don't want any stealing going on.

So what would you do? If thievery is your game and you prefer not to be caught, then you might go to some other store. But if you were playing a more horrific game, perhaps you were planning to explode a bomb in the store, then you wouldn't care about the camera. The reason for this is simple: You don't care about being caught, and the camera will probably be destroyed in the explosion anyhow.

Note also that if the store owners really wanted to catch you, then they would have hidden the camera. Perhaps you've even seen the types of stealth cameras that can be hidden in clocks, pens, watches, or even Christmas ornaments.[38] So keep this in mind: Surveillance cameras producing logs in stealth mode are not meant to keep people honest , they're meant to catch people being dishonest.

To better understand the use of log files for security, let's examine what happens when you are trying to get money at an ATM machine. It's pretty familiar: You step up to the machine, slide in your card, and then type in your personal identification number (PIN).

As you do all of this, the ATM has a computer system located off on the network somewhere. This system produces a log file of your activity. Entries in the file will show that you slid in your card at such-and-such a time, and that you successfully typed in your PIN at such-and-such a time after that. The log file will also show that you took out some money and left.

As long as you behave, everything will be just fine in the logs. But what if the log file showed that you tried seventeen different PINs and then took your card back and left? What would security analysts conclude if they were reviewing the logs?

---

[38] An ornament camera poses an interesting dilemma: If it is ugly, it will be placed at the back of the tree where surveillance is poor, so it has to be pretty.

They might think that a thief was trying to guess your PIN, or that you simply forgot your PIN, or perhaps that the ATM machine was not working properly. All of these are perfectly reasonable possibilities and all demonstrate the difficulties associated with processing audit logs.

A couple of years ago, I was waiting in line at the local supermarket. I had two carts worth of groceries and my kids were being particularly fidgety that day. I think it was Christmastime, so the supermarket was really jammed. There were probably ten carts behind me.

Once everything was in bags, I pulled out my ATM card, the supermarket had just installed this system, and I scanned it in. The little device asked me for my PIN, and to my horror, I couldn't remember it. I realized at the time how contextual one's memory can be: That is, whenever I lean out of the window in my car, my PIN rolls off my fingers like silk. But there in the supermarket with those mean people behind me glaring at me, and my kids being so bad, I just couldn't remember it.

So what did I do? I started guessing. Ten guesses into my sweaty ordeal, it occurred to me that if the ATM system had a team of security analysts watching the log files as they were produced, I would be dead. My guesses looked just like hacking. Eventually, I did get the right PIN, to the cashier's amazement, and I escaped the incident unscathed.

Here's another log file story: I started my career in the mid-1980's working on a secure Unix-based operating system called System V/MLS. I've alluded to this system several times throughout this book. The system was built around an amazing piece of core Unix software designed by Chuck Flink at Bell Labs.

Anyway, that Unix system included an awesome security log file capability, one that hackers would never be able to trip up because it was cleverly protected in the operating system. During a computer security convention in Washington, we had our monitors propped up in front of our booth and we couldn't wait for the people to come by and look at this feature.

Unfortunately, people seemed to be bunching around our competitor's booth. We knew that they had an inferior system, but everyone was crowded around their table gawking. Now, it's usually bad manners to go over to your competitor's booth, but we just couldn't stand it. So we walked over and found that they had done something really clever: The output of their logging system had been formatted to look like a New York Stock Exchange ticker tape.

Today, too few security managers set up their systems to produce and process logs. This is a terrific shame, because almost all software, computers, and networks already have the ability to create such a record of observed activity. Sometimes, this record is called a history. Sometimes, it's called an audit trail. Sometimes, it's called a log file. Sometimes it's called accounting.

In any event, it's there. And we will refer to the gathering of data in this manner as collection. In one of the most publicized security incidents ever, Cliff Stoll from Lawrence Berkeley Labs chased down and caught a West German hacker who'd been breaking into United states Federal Government computers. Here's what Stoll had to say about logs:

"Our logbook reflected both confusion and progress," he says – referring in this case to manual logs in a book, "but eventually pointed the way to the solution." I really like this notion of pointing the way to the solution, because that is what logs allow.

And yet, the infrastructure does not exist in most companies or nations to make effective use of this collected evidence. "It is not surprising to find that the automated audit trail record keeping has been completely turned off," write security experts Andrew Blythe and Gerald Kovacich.

This paradox is comparable to installing an expensive surveillance camera and deciding not to turn it on. This must change because the adequate processing of log files is a powerful means for protecting infrastructure from cyber attack. New tools called threat management systems now exist to allow for more efficient processing of this information. One can only hope that the use of threat management increases, especially in critical infrastructure environments.

Summary
Of
Key Points

Throughout the book, we have highlighted various key points that underscore particularly important issues in cyber security. For convenience, I list these various points here, in the order in which they appeared in the book.

An effective way to attack critical infrastructure is to target the underlying software, computers, and networks.

During a period of seeming quiet, never confuse good luck with improved cyber security.

Interoperability and common computing environments make cyber attacks easier.

No justification exists for intentional Easter Eggs or Trojan horses, however innocent, to be placed in software by developers.

It is generally not possible for a government or any other group to determine accurately the true source of a cyber attack.

The most valuable contribution government can make to cyber security involves providing incentives for software makers to create more correct code.

Flaws in software can allow wide open doors for malicious intruders.

Twenty years ago, we didn't know how to connect computers. Today, we don't know how to separate them.

Virtually every computer can be reached over a network from any other computer.

Authenticating remote access to an enterprise network must involve something other than a password.

Business managers make their most substantive contribution to increased cyber security by enforcing policy.

Index